THE OVERCOMERS

GOD'S VISION FOR YOU TO THRIVE
IN AN AGE OF ANXIETY AND OUTRAGE

MATT CHANDLER

W PUBLISHING GROUP

AN IMPRINT OF THOMAS NELSON

Published in Nashville, Tennessee, by W Publishing, an imprint of Thomas Nelson.

Published in association with Yates & Yates, www.yates2.com.

Thomas Nelson titles may be purchased in bulk for educational, business, fundraising, or sales promotional use. For information, please email SpecialMarkets@ThomasNelson.com.

Unless otherwise noted, Scripture quotations are taken from the ESV® Bible (The Holy Bible, English Standard Version®). Copyright © 2001 by Crossway, a publishing ministry of Good News Publishers. Used by permission. All rights reserved.

Scripture quotations marked NIV are taken from The Holy Bible, New International Version®, NIV®. Copyright © 1973, 1978, 1984, 2011 by Biblica, Inc.® Used by permission of Zondervan. All rights reserved worldwide. www.Zondervan.com. The "NIV" and "New International Version" are trademarks registered in the United States Patent and Trademark Office by Biblica, Inc.®

Italics added to direct Scripture quotations are the author's emphasis.

Any internet addresses, phone numbers, or company or product information printed in this book are offered as a resource and are not intended in any way to be or to imply an endorsement by Thomas Nelson, nor does Thomas Nelson vouch for the existence, content, or services of these sites, phone numbers, companies, or products beyond the life of this book.

ISBN 978-1-4003-4429-1 (audiobook)
ISBN 978-1-4003-4428-4 (ePub)
ISBN 978-1-4003-4426-0 (HC)
ISBN 978-1-4003-4517-5 (ITPE)

Library of Congress Control Number: 2023950125

Printed in the United States of America
24 25 26 27 28 LBC 5 4 3 2 1

THE
OVERCOMERS

To the Overcomers at The Village Church.
You embody all I have written here!

CONTENTS

INTRODUCTION

GOD'S SURPRISING PLAN TO
PUSH BACK DARKNESS

What if I told you that you are made for this exact moment in human history? That it's not just blue check mark, celebrity Christians we need at this moment, but *you*. Not the future version of you or the person you hope to become, but *you now*! Would you roll your eyes and think, *Yeah, yeah, Pastor Matt. Sure I am.*

Or would you believe me?

What if I told you that you can be braver than you think? That you can be more confident and that you're dangerous when it comes to the enemy's work in our day? Could I convince you that you're uniquely wired and placed in this moment in human history as part of God's big plan to push back the darkness and establish light?

Not me, Matt. I'm no Mother Teresa.

You don't know my story, Matt. I'm actually a mess.

You're a pastor. You have to say that.

Yada yada . . .

What if I told you that you don't need to be anxious or afraid of anything? Would you trust me if I told you that you're not a victim and don't have to be a passive bystander?

I realize this might be hard to believe, but you're a crucial part of what God is working out in our day.

YOU ARE AN OVERCOMER

I wish we were sitting together talking over a cup of coffee at Marty B's Coffee down the road from me. I'd love to hear how God has been at work in your life and how He's led you to this book. Over a strong, long black, I'd ask you what you were hoping for when you picked it up and began reading. We'd talk about the curiosities, the stories, the doubts, and the lies you're dealing with at this very moment. Knowing these things about you would lead me to press harder on certain parts of this book and not as hard on others. There would be moments we would take a break or veer into a tangent. Or maybe we'd stop and pray or cry or laugh. Unfortunately, I don't have the luxury of sitting in person and conversing with you. It really is my preferred pastime to sit with other believers and share our stories.

And so, I write today as best I can as one who knows the Bible, as a fellow sojourner in this Christian life, and as a pastor who has witnessed the masterful ways our enemy deceives and lies to us, hoping we shrink back from the dynamic, empowered life God intends for us—the life we want for ourselves.

Despite what you and I may see, God is at work in the mess of our world and our everyday lives. Believe it or not, God is accomplishing His purposes: He is seeking and saving the lost. He is exacting justice on His creation. He is working miracles among the sick and brokenhearted. He is pouring out His grace and forgiveness on all of us.

At this very moment, God is calling people into a deeper relationship with Him—one that is built on the power and authority of Jesus. And here's the crazy part: you have been called right into the center of this ultimate reality.

Do you realize you belong to a global people who have thrived through worldwide pandemics, peacefully overthrown tyrannical empires, increased the safety and dignity of women and children around the world, and ushered in the end of a global slave trade? What if I told you that many of our nation's hospitals and orphanages have denominational names because your spiritual family cared for the sick and looked after the widows and orphans in their distress?

Your spiritual family pushed back the darkness and established order and light, even as they fought to overcome their own sins and doubts for two thousand years. It's your turn now, and you have it in you. Here is a definition of an Overcomer I've pulled from the Scriptures:

An Overcomer is a believer propelled by scriptural truths, empowered by the work of Jesus, and encouraged by those who have gone before them. With open eyes to deeper spiritual realities, the one who overcomes endures the brokenness of the world with holy resolve. This individual, marked by love and through the power of the Holy Spirit, joins in God's offensive against darkness and destruction. The Overcomer unites with the triune God and His holy church to stand as an unwavering, unanxious presence. Bluntly put, the Overcomer is a major problem to the enemy.

During the past two thousand years, there have been extremely difficult times when our spiritual family could have wilted, fled for the hills, or silently ignored the world's pains. But God, knowing it's scary to be us, let us in on a picture of ultimate reality in the book of Revelation. That picture has put steel in the spines of our brothers and sisters across time and space, and it does the same for us today. So as you flip through the pages of this book, I want to show you this picture of ultimate reality, your place in God's divine purposes, and why Satan is terrified that you have this book in your hands.

In 1933, James J. Braddock was a has-been boxer who had lost a heavyweight title fight and never fully recovered. Had we met him that year, we would think almost everything about him was unimpressive. He was working as a longshoreman with an impaired right hand and a face that looked like he'd been smacked with a frying pan. He was trying to survive the Great Depression by working on the docks and was not really succeeding. Braddock was forced to go on government relief in an attempt to support his family.

In 1934, Braddock was given a fight against a promising and highly touted fighter named John "Corn" Griffin, whom he knocked out in the third round. After several other wins, it became apparent that not only had Braddock's right hand healed, but his left was now stronger from his work on the docks. On June 13, 1935, in the Madison Square Garden Bowl, Braddock, a ten-to-one underdog, fought the younger, stronger, and faster heavyweight champion of the world, Max Baer, and won. In what was called one of the "greatest fistic upsets" of his time, James J. Braddock, nicknamed "Cinderella Man," revealed he was stronger than people thought and had more untapped potential than anyone could have imagined.[1]

Throughout the history of the church, we have too many Cinderella men and women to count. We can easily rattle off the famous ones: the apostle John, Peter, Paul, Mary Magdalene, John the Baptist, Augustine, Martin Luther, Corrie ten Boom, John Wycliffe,

John Calvin, John Wesley, C. S. Lewis, Dietrich Bonhoeffer, Florence Nightingale, Billy Graham.

But there are exponentially more obscure, remarkable, honorable, godly Christian leaders you haven't heard of. Millions, actually. Maybe you know a believer in your life, past or present, who has significantly influenced you. All these Christians were uniquely made and placed for their time for a specific God-orchestrated reason.

PAUL, I'VE HEARD OF

There's a fascinating story in Acts 19 about a group of itinerant Jewish exorcists (who knew that was a thing?) who started using the name of Jesus in an attempt to cast out demons after watching the apostle Paul do all sorts of miracles. Starting in verse 11, the passage reads:

> And God was doing extraordinary miracles by the hands of Paul, so that even handkerchiefs or aprons that had touched his skin were carried away to the sick, and their diseases left them and the evil spirits came out of them. Then some of the itinerant Jewish exorcists undertook to invoke the name of the Lord Jesus over those who had evil spirits, saying, "I adjure you by the Jesus whom Paul proclaims." Seven sons of a Jewish high priest named Sceva were doing this. But the evil spirit answered them, "Jesus I know, and Paul I recognize, but who are you?" (vv. 11–15)

Did you catch that? "Jesus I know, and *Paul I recognize*." I love that passage. Paul was wreaking so much havoc in Satan's kingdom that the demons basically said, "We've heard of him." Can you picture word spreading about Paul throughout the domain of darkness as the demons told one another about this punk guy who had been causing them all kinds of problems?

If I may put all my cards on the table here at the very beginning, this is what I'm calling you to boldly step into—to become a problem for the enemy! In the spaces you live, work, and play, you, too, can be a dynamic disrupter of the powers of this present darkness—so much that the demons recognize you (as they did Paul) as a threat to their evil plans and schemes.

More than likely, at this moment, you want to interrupt me and explain that you're no apostle Paul. Here's the thing: I know you're not. Neither am I. You're you, and I'm me. That's important because these are *our* days, not Paul's. He had his days; these are ours. God's big plan for today is *you*. Not Paul or Peter or Augustine or Charles Spurgeon or Billy Graham. You!

To understand the fullness of who we are and what our purpose is, you and I need to consider ourselves in three ways:

1. We are made in the image of God.
2. We are children of God.
3. We are uniquely wired and uniquely placed by God.

It's vital to understand we are all three of these things before we are able to step into our design and destiny and embrace what we were fully intended to be.

There's a simple, important fact: we are made in God's image. This sets us apart from the rest of creation. Though we are not God, we were created to reflect Him in ways only humans can. As Christians, we are also children of God, adopted into His family and fellow heirs with Christ. This intimacy as His children provides special access to the Father, who delights in us. As we better understand this truth, we are able to become our true selves and recognize our true worth. This is why I ask you to consider whether we're being led by the Spirit and attempting to obey Jesus' call on our lives. While we won't do it perfectly, is obedience our desire? As children of God, it is. And as children of God, we are offered a special connection with Him. He is for us and always with us. He knows us and defends us. Even in hard times or when we're struggling with sin, the Holy Spirit is there, guiding us and offering His comfort and mercy. I then want to remind you that we are at war with the enemy, who wants to undermine God's good plan for our lives. Satan uses our wounds, painful experiences, and tendency to compare to keep us from living in God's will. But we are not the first ones to deal with this, and I invite you to walk through the book of Revelation with me as we embrace God's purpose for us.

CHAPTER 1

MORE POWERFUL THAN YOU BELIEVE

On Sunday mornings, I usually get up several hours earlier than anyone else in our home. My crew goes to our church's 11 a.m. service, and they are happily asleep when my alarm goes off around 5 a.m. So I grope around in the dark for clothes and shoes. I'm not fashion-forward or trendy, so it's not overly imperative that I get the right outfit. I have what my wife, Lauren, calls "a uniform"—jeans, a button-up or polo, and boots.

If I'm wearing a button-up, I pull down the shirt and make sure I get the bottom button right. If I don't, the shirt looks janky and certainly would distract the congregation as I preached. So I want to start our journey in this book with the bottom button.

YOU ARE MADE IN GOD'S IMAGE

The first thing you must understand is simple: *you are made in God's image.*

This fact alone makes you spectacularly distinct from the rest of creation. It's not just that you are different and more valuable than every other animal. You're also separate from inanimate objects like the land, sky, and stars.

But as an image bearer, what makes you so incredible is that, according to Genesis 1:26–27, you are like God somehow.

> "Let us make man in our image, after our likeness. And let them have dominion over the fish of the sea and over the birds of the heavens and over the livestock and over all the earth and over every creeping thing that creeps on the earth."
>
> So God created man in his own image, in the image of God he created him; male and female he created them.

Think about that. You are somehow like the Creator God of the universe. Keep in mind that being like God is very different than being God Himself. But you were created to reflect the God of the universe simply *in your being.*

YOU ARE A CHILD OF GOD

The next thing you need to understand is that if you're a Christian, you are a child of God, adopted by the blood of Jesus into the family of God with all the rights and privileges of belonging to God's family. You are an heir of God and fellow heir with Christ. This is your primary identity. More than being a husband or wife, friend, mother or father, son or daughter, lawyer or graphic designer, or welder or teacher. You get the point—*you are a child of God.*

You are with Jesus, and He is with you. You have access to the Father and to "every spiritual blessing in the heavenly places" (Ephesians 1:3). Every other false identity or projected image of yourself that you might latch onto to give you confidence, security, or reassurance can be stolen from you. But the fact is, you belong to God, and He won't ever let you go.

But there's more: as your heavenly Father, *God delights in you.*

Don't roll your eyes. I'm serious.

God delights in you, not because of anything you have accomplished but because of who you are, His child. If you're a parent, you know the deep love you have for your children, even on their worst days.

God doesn't regret saving you either. He isn't in love with the future you, the person you might become. He cherishes you right now with all your disappointments and dramas, doubts and fears, anxieties and anger. He sees you, He knows where He's leading you, and He is all-in on His glory being revealed in you. I would call this your general identity.[1]

This is excellent news because you don't have to create a version of yourself or seek to define yourself in a particular way. God created you, and God will define you! We'll talk more about this later, but the more you understand that you are His child, the more you become yourself—your *true self.*

Accepting and embracing your general identity as a child of God and believing it in your gut is the first step in recognizing your true worth. Everything else about you and how God sees you, designed you, and has placed you today hinges on your understanding that you are made in His image and appointed an heir to His kingdom.

CHILD OF GOD

If you have trouble understanding your identity as a child of God, let me take you to one of the dozens of passages that reveal this truth.[2]

Romans 8 is the Mount Everest of chapters in the Bible. The Holy Spirit takes us to the heights of life in the Spirit, our future glory, and God's everlasting love through the apostle Paul, who wrote, "And we know that for those who love God all things work together for good, for those who are called according to his purpose" (v. 28).

Just before these epic and beautiful truths, we read these four verses:

> For all who are led by the Spirit of God are sons of God. For you did not receive the spirit of slavery to fall back into fear, but you have received the Spirit of adoption as sons, by whom we cry, "Abba! Father!" The Spirit himself bears witness with our spirit that we are children of God, and if children, then heirs—heirs of God and fellow heirs with Christ, provided we suffer with him in order that we may also be glorified with him. (Romans 8:14–17)

Look again at the first part of that passage: "All who are led by the Spirit of God are sons of God" (v. 14). Paul used the masculine word *son* here because the firstborn son was the heir in his day. If you're my sister in Christ, he's talking about you here too. A funny way I talk about these passages at the church I pastor is that if I get to be the bride of Christ as a man, then you women get to be sons when it comes to inheritance.

So let me ask you: Are you being led by the Spirit? Are you attempting to follow Jesus and obey His call on your life?

Notice I didn't ask whether you think you are doing it perfectly or

4

even if you are doing it well in this season of your life. The question is, Do you desire to follow Jesus, and are you at this moment doing the best you know how with where you currently are in life? Do you have affection for Jesus and a desire to follow Him more fully and faithfully? If you are, and if you do, then you are being led by the Spirit. And what does Romans 8 say about you? You are a child of God.

The next verse tells us what we can expect as children of God: we no longer have "the spirit of slavery" that makes us "fall back into fear" (v. 15). Before we were sons of God, we were slaves to the opinions of others, our own desires, lifeless religion, and what the Bible calls "the world." This life led to fear—fear of rejection, fear of failure, fear of being found out as a fraud, and fear of not being enough. But not anymore!

Paul went on to say that we "have received the Spirit of adoption as sons, by whom we cry, 'Abba! Father!'" (v. 15). When we understand we are children of God, we should no longer be afraid. Maybe you have a friend who addresses God as "Daddy God" or "Papa God" or something like that. That's likely because they've been told that *Abba* is the equivalent of *Daddy*. But *Abba* is even bigger than *Daddy*. It contains a sense of deep intimacy but also of great power. It's more like, "My dad can beat up your dad."

This intimate connection with God is in view near the end of Romans 8 when Paul asked four big questions:

1. "If God is for us, who can be against us?" (v. 31).
2. "Who shall bring any charge against God's elect?" (v. 33).
3. "Who is to condemn?" (v. 34).
4. "Who shall separate us from the love of Christ?" (v. 35).

These are big Daddy questions reserved for a mighty Abba Father. If God is your Abba Father, who could possibly be against you? Who could possibly bring any charge against you? Your Dad has justified you. Your Dad knows everything about you.

- God knows you better than you know yourself, and He hasn't condemned you. Who then could possibly condemn you?
- How have you experienced your Dad? Who could possibly separate you from His love?
- Don't you see how powerful God is? How committed He is to you? How much He delights in you?
- Why are you a slave to fear when you are His child?

God knows these truths are hard for you and me to believe. We can believe these realities about others, but it's hard to fully embrace them about ourselves. That's why Paul wrote, "The Spirit himself bears witness with our spirit that we are children of God" (v. 16). Even when things aren't great in your life, the Spirit is *with* you, helping you to know you're a child of God.

One way you can sense the Spirit with you is when you feel the bittersweet conviction over your sin. Not just guilt but the sweetness of conviction that you failed Jesus even as He loves you. Yes, this is God at work in your life. Conviction is the Spirit testifying that you're a child of God. It's an invitation into what's ultimately better—obedience and grace. Your Abba Father doesn't want you to live in sin; He wants to spare you the consequences of sin, and He actively pursues you to bring you back to Himself. Men and women who aren't children of God don't feel the conviction of the Spirit. Instead, they feel guilt or shame or ambivalence and passivity.

What about divine affection? Do you have a longing and desire to love Jesus more deeply and follow Him more faithfully? My guess is that you are reading this book because you want to fan into flame your love for Jesus. You want to be an Overcomer! That's the Spirit testifying to your spirit that you're a child of God.

Or what about joy? During hard seasons, whether in pain or long-suffering, when circumstances are overwhelming and everything feels like a struggle, are you somehow able to experience a supernatural joy and peace? Is there a core belief in your heart and mind that the God of the universe is still on the throne, looking out for you, and His way is perfect and unfailing? That's the Spirit testifying that you are His.

As mentioned earlier, Paul said that if we are God's children, we're "heirs of God and fellow heirs with Christ" (Romans 8:17). What does this mean? You will reign and rule alongside Jesus forever in a remade heaven and earth—an earth where the mountains produce sweet wine, where the wolf and lamb take naps together, and where the lion chews hay rather than devouring the antelope. The Bible says the deserts will bloom with flowers, and there will be no more weeping, pain, or loss.

That's a pretty epic inheritance, but it isn't the central piece. You will also inherit a resurrected body. That might not sound like a big deal to you if you're young and strong, but I'm at that age where even sleeping can cause an injury. This new body you have coming for you doesn't get sick, break, age, or die.

But the best part of our inheritance is that you get God! Unfettered, face-to-face, and pulled right into the eternal, perfect dance of love of the triune God of the universe. You get ever-increasing joy in the presence of your Savior. It'd be worthless if you got everything else but didn't get Him. Paul reminded you there are massive benefits to being God's child in the here and now, but just you wait; the best is on its way.

The last line of Romans 8:17—"provided we suffer with him in order that we may also be glorified with him"—is a phrase that most of us wish wasn't there. Yet, if it wasn't, the Scriptures wouldn't line up with our reality.

God loves us too much not to let us know we'll have trouble in this world. I've argued in other places that what you see in the Bible isn't clean and stable lives, but messy, complicated, broken people with God right in the middle of every day—sustaining, encouraging, and reminding them of His grace. Because you're a child of God, you're not under wrath, but under mercy. Our inheritance and our suffering are linked together.

When suffering comes, regardless of its form, you can look to your heavenly Father, who loves you and has not abandoned you. Repeatedly in the Scriptures, the Bible paints the picture of an enemy trying to destroy a loving God, but He cannot be conquered. Our Abba Father always outmaneuvers the devil's plans and redeems them, and us, for His glory.

John Newton, the former slave trader turned abolitionist and writer of the hymn "Amazing Grace," told the following story to help us see our suffering through the lens of our inheritance:

> Suppose a man was going to New York to take possession of a large estate, and his [carriage] should break down a mile before he got to the city, which obliged him to walk the rest of the way; what a fool we should think him if we saw him wringing his hands, and blubbering out all the remaining mile, "My [carriage] is broken! My [carriage] is broken!"[3]

I know life can be difficult and outright painful, but we will inherit a large estate one day. We can acknowledge our hard days and be honest about our hurts and disappointments, but we shouldn't disparage the difficult days because of what we've already gained as heirs.

I'm not just talking about eternity either. Our faith in Christ is an immediate reward we gain the minute we acknowledge and accept Jesus as Lord.

UNIQUELY WIRED,
UNIQUELY PLACED

For years, I had a picture on my refrigerator of me with two of my heroes: J. I. Packer and John Piper. During my early walk with Christ, God used these two men in a powerful and formative way. My wife, Lauren, would sometimes joke with a wink that I looked happier in that picture than I did in some of our wedding photos. I wasn't, but the truth is, for many years, these two leaders were the picture of what I aspired to be.

They were examples of how I was to live, lead, pastor, and preach. I'd double down and write out my sermons word for word, suppress my personality while preaching to avoid drawing attention to myself, and parrot and quote these men incessantly. Over the years of emulating, a weariness set in, and I started to feel constrained and frustrated. I had taken it too far. Rather than becoming a sanctified version of myself, I had become a cheaper, less-gifted version of them.

Finding my unique voice, style, and wiring was one of the more thrilling seasons of my life and has led to an immense sense of joy and purpose. Can you relate? Do you compare yourself to your best friend, wishing you could mother your children the way she mothers hers? Do you wish you had *his* charisma, *her* patience, *his* organizational skills, or *her* quiet strength? It's one thing to desire these characteristics, but have you gone so far as to try to copycat them, becoming some version of *them* instead of the authentic version of *you*?

The enemy likes it very much when we try to be a knockoff of other people rather than growing into the people God has designed us to be. But the fact is, we don't need more of the same. The world needs faithful, committed followers of Jesus who are brave and bold enough to live and serve as their authentic, God-crafted selves. There's no one like you, with your DNA, fingerprints, taste buds, curiosities and temptations, exact thoughts and feelings, gifts and talents, perspectives and experiences. And since no one in the entire world is identical to you, you are unique and special.

In Psalm 139, David began to marvel at God's handiwork in his life and how God had put him together. Starting in verse 13, he said:

> For you formed my inward parts;
>> you knitted me together in my mother's womb.
>> I praise you, for I am fearfully and wonderfully made.
>> Wonderful are your works;
>> my soul knows it very well.
>> My frame was not hidden from you,
>> when I was being made in secret,
>> intricately woven in the depths of the earth.
>> Your eyes saw my unformed substance;
>> in your book were written, every one of them,
>> the days that were formed for me,
>> when as yet there was none of them. (vv. 13–16)

David started by saying God knit him together in his mother's womb. David used poetry to convey the idea that God is up to something underneath the biology of baby making. As Christians, we know the science behind conception. We know where babies come from, but we don't think about how God might be up to something underneath the science.

This idea isn't just true of David; it's true of you. God knit you together in your mother's womb. He didn't accidentally screw up when he gave you that birthmark, learning disability, or genetic marker.

David wasn't content with generalities either. He marveled at specifics. He said, "My frame was not hidden from you" (v. 15). David was speaking of our physical bodies—God is involved all the way down to our recessive and dominant genes.

Anyone who has been around me or heard me preach knows that I'm a loud person. I have what my mom calls "a voice that carries." When I was young, my loud voice consistently got me in trouble. My booming voice would lead to detention halls, the loss of privileges, and the occasional spanking. Ironically, what I used to get in trouble for, I now somewhat do for a living.

To make matters worse, I'm six foot five. The most consistent thing people say about me is that I'm taller than expected. Most weeks of the year, I preach multiple times. I can project, and my voice has rarely weakened or gone out on me. I see my height and loud voice as things God wove into my frame in my mother's womb because they give me a unique presence as I preach and teach. He had a plan for me and dialed in the correct genes.

What about you? Do you have distinguishing characteristics that show God's hand at work?

It's not just your frame that God designed and built. David also wrote that "inward parts" (v. 13) and "unformed substance" (v. 16) make us who we are. I think this has to do with our personality and natural tendencies. I have three children: Audrey, Reid, and Norah. Each was unique from the moment they were born. One was easygoing and rarely bothered, one was needy and hard to comfort, and the other was marked by unwavering joy.

So David was saying God's in that stuff too. Are you naturally extroverted or introverted? Are you past-oriented or future-oriented?

Lauren and I are different. I'm an extrovert who is future-oriented. She can be extroverted but needs quality time by herself before and after being in crowds. Lauren is also past-oriented. When she wakes up in the morning, she isn't thinking about what needs to be done that day. She's thinking of a conversation she had the day before or something someone said at dinner a week ago. I've never woken up with that kind of thing on my mind. I wake up thinking of what needs to be done and when I'll get to do the things that need to get done. I'm playful to a fault, and I like meeting new people. David was saying God is in that too!

What are you like? What have you been like your whole life? Can you remember what you were like before you started pretending and copycatting who you think you're *supposed* to be?

Okay, I want to stop for a second to ensure we don't get confused by what we're trying to do here. I'm not trying to convince you of these things for your self-esteem. God is doing this. God formed your frame. God designed your unformed substance. God dialed in the perfect mix of all the genetic possibilities around your personhood. God made you uniquely you.

As incredible as you are, you are God's handiwork *for a purpose*. What is He up to? In verse 16, David said God weaves that unformed substance together with the view of "the days that were formed for [you], when as yet there was none of them." God made you for these days and these days for you, literally. The apostle Paul grabbed hold of this idea in Ephesians 2:10 when he called you God's poetry and said He created good works for you to do.

It's not just that you are uniquely wired; you're also exactly where you're meant to be for now. You are uniquely placed.

In Acts 17, the apostle Paul gave what I believe was his most comprehensive sermon. Standing in the epicenter of Athenian politics and religions, Paul said:

> And he made from one man every nation of mankind to live on all the face of the earth, having determined allotted periods and the boundaries of their dwelling place, that they should seek God, and perhaps feel their way toward him and find him. Yet he is actually not far from each one of us. (vv. 26–27)

Notice that Paul said God has "determined allotted periods and the boundaries of [our] dwelling place" (v. 26). Simply put, you are not an accident. Your parents' family planning has no bearing on your being here. God had an allotted time for you. That time is now. I said this earlier, and I'll say it again. This is *your* day, *your* time. Not Moses' or David's or Peter's or Paul's. Ours. Yours. We were made for this day, and this day was made for us!

Do you like where you live? What's your favorite part about it? I live in the Dallas–Ft. Worth metroplex in the middle of what is considered a suburban sprawl. In the sprawl, the natural beauty is harder to see—unless you count the numerous Chick-fil-As. It's not Whitefish, Montana, or Jackson Hole, Wyoming, but this is where I am called in this season of my life. God has uniquely wired me and placed me in my physical location in His redemptive plans for this moment.

I also want to point out that Paul said you are uniquely placed so that people "should seek God, and perhaps feel their way toward him and find him. Yet he is actually not far from each one of us" (v. 27). Did you read that? You've been uniquely wired and placed so that people might seek Him and find Him. There's a divine purpose to how you were made, the time you were created, and where you were placed.

AT WAR

Two great forces have been at play in your life. We've covered the first one: your heavenly Father made you for the day and the days for you. However, another evil force has also been in your life from the beginning. He is our great enemy. The Bible calls him Satan but also mentions demonic principalities and powers (Ephesians 6:12), in addition to our flesh (Romans 7:14) and what is called "the world" (John 15:19).

We know Satan is a liar. Jesus said, "When he lies, he speaks out of his own character, for he is a liar and the father of lies" (John 8:44). One thing I'm certain of is that we've all been lied to our whole lives. When we believe those lies, we create what the apostle Paul called "strongholds" (2 Corinthians 10:4). Strongholds are mindsets, value systems, or thought processes that hinder us from growing into God's design and destiny for our lives. Satan is serious about getting you to play small, and he does that by whispering doubts about God's goodness and ability into the deep parts of your soul.

There are three main ways Satan tries to twist our perception of our unique design with his lies. The first is through words and wounds, the second is through comparison, and lastly, through an attempt at perfection. Strongholds take hold of us, but if we're not careful, we'll also take hold of them. They can make us feel safe or in control even as they disrupt and destroy our lives.

WORDS AND WOUNDS

My family started going to counseling when I was six years old. I can't remember if it was voluntary or required, but I remember going several times. The reason for that counseling had nothing to do with me, but as I sat in that room, a thought began to form in my young heart: I had caused everyone in my family to need counseling.

I was a fairly hyper and loud kid and was already getting into trouble. Over the next couple of years, this idea morphed into, *You mess things up, people will be able to put up with you for only a little while before they leave you, and you're hard to deal with.* These thoughts grew up with me and became my internal operating system, subconsciously shaping my external world.

It took nearly thirty years before I figured out those thoughts were short-circuiting certain areas of my life. Only with some deep, painful work with a trusted counselor and faithful friendships did I recognize it and see that stronghold break. This is how the enemy works. He knows that you—the real you—were made for the day, so he comes in through a wound or a careless word spoken over you. He aims to paralyze and destroy you, to permanently crush your spirit so that you lay down your weapons and give in.

For me, the stronghold began by utterly misreading a situation that had nothing to do with me. Maybe for you, the stronghold came through the wounds done *to you* that were real and horrific. As a pastor, I've heard devastating and demonic stories of neglect, abuse, violence, and rape. Satan is the author of such things, and he torments the victim with lies, multiplying the effect of the violence.

Here's the truth: you are not the thing that happened to you. And you are not to blame for the evil perpetrated against you. Satan wants you stuck in regret, self-hatred, and self-blame—defined by that moment. He doesn't want you to experience redemption and healing. And he certainly doesn't want you restored and weaponized against your true enemy. He's desperate to get you either to isolate or join a community of bitterness and revenge rather than redemption and release.

Now, I'm not telling you not to be angry about what's happened to you. I don't think you can heal if you bury anger, and I believe God is equally furious over the way His child was treated. But you can trust God to handle the person who sinned against you, and His judgment is fierce and eternal. I want to help you release and hand over to God what is His. We aren't meant to carry such a heavy weight.

Too often we clothe ourselves with our trauma to our own destruction. I plead with you not to define yourself by that painful experience. I've watched God take some of the worst pain imaginable, heal the person, and redeem the moment by weaponizing it to help others who've suffered similar pain. God can redeem what the enemy used in an attempt to destroy you.

COMPARISON, THE THIEF OF GRATITUDE

Several years ago, our oldest daughter was caught up in some teenage girl drama. Teenage girls can be so cruel. They can go after the soul and pulverize it. One of the girls in the drama said that Audrey was the "Walmart version" of this other girl.

I'm not sure what this young lady has against Walmart, but her point was to say that Audrey was a cheaper version of this other young woman. It was supposed to be a burn, but she stumbled onto some truth in her attempt to be mean. If Audrey were attempting to be this other girl, she would've certainly been a cheaper version of her.

Audrey is Audrey. I am me, and you are you. Satan wants us to compare ourselves to others, whether better or worse. He wants to draw our attention away from what God has said about us and for us to interpret our value based on the people around us, not on God's truth. Satan knows the more we become like Jesus, the more we become ourselves. The more clearly we see Jesus, the more clearly we see who we really are reflected in our identity as His children. That would make us a real problem for the devil's schemes and strategies because the last thing Satan wants is for us to walk in confidence and security as ourselves. He wants each of us to think, *There's something wrong with me.*

Comparison robs us of a life of gratitude and makes us more like Satan, whom the Bible calls the "accuser of our brothers" (Revelation 12:10). When I say "life of gratitude," I'm talking about being grateful for your personhood, not your possessions. I'm talking about gratitude that God made you *you*. It's not arrogant to be grateful for how God has wired you and marvel at how He uses you. It's an overcorrection away from the current cult of expressive individualism to hate yourself or fail to acknowledge that God has been significantly at work in your life.

I don't know what you've been through, but God does, and you're still here. You have a book in your hand, and you're fighting. I think that's amazing. By the end of this book, I hope you're not just hanging in there but rather causing all kinds of problems for the powers and principalities of this present darkness.

You need to be vigilant against the near-constant bombardment of images and advertisements meant to provoke comparison and discontentment in your heart. I'm not anti-tech or anti-social media, but I encourage you to pay attention to what happens to your soul as you scroll. Comparison and self-hate aren't just things you do; they are accusations against God. Accusations that He hasn't been good to you, that He made a mistake in how He uniquely wired and uniquely placed you.

EMBRACING IMPERFECTION

The only perfect person who has ever lived is Jesus of Nazareth. You already know this, but let me remind you anyway. No one else has come close to perfection. No matter a person's exploits or stunning abilities, we're all a mixture of shadow and light, gold and dust. Our great enemy wants you stuck in a very real spiritual paralysis because you happen to be an imperfect human.

But remember, God wants to use your natural abilities and spiritual gifts for a purpose. If the enemy can get you stuck in fear over faith and have you believing that other people can do what God has given you to do better than you can, he can ultimately take you out of the fight. Perfectionism has us living in fear, forgetting that God doesn't measure success by outcomes but by bold faith. It's faith that pleases God. When our perfectionism has us deciding that our lives and actions won't make that much difference or that others with more talent are doing it better, we become spectators rather than participants in the universe's greatest drama.

I know these are challenging times. I hope things will change soon, but that's above my pay grade.

We aren't the first generation of Christians to deal with massive moral, social, and national issues. For over two thousand years now, there have been various levels of hostility toward and cooperation with Christians and the social, moral order of the day. Some generations were fed to the lions, and others were given stunning amounts of influence in all domains of society.

You and I are in a time of increasing hostility and marginalization of Christians in America, but I've seen too much of the world to call it outright persecution. We're definitely out of fashion and a continued nuisance to the culture.

How have the generations of believers before us not only held fast but thrived? How did our brothers and sisters overcome the brutality of the Roman Empire and hold on to holiness during the Dark Ages? How do Christians continue to overcome in countries like China, Iran, and other places where devotion to Christ could get you killed?

Until the last one hundred and fifty years or so, Christians have been emboldened and strengthened by the book of Revelation. I know that might surprise you. Unfortunately, many believers think Revelation is too scary or too weird to understand today. Yet it has provided the strength and courage God's people have needed throughout history to help them not shrink back but live bold and courageous lives regardless of the times.

So I want to look through the book of Revelation to encourage you as you embrace your design and destiny. If you happen to fall into the category of those who view Revelation as intimidating or too strange to understand, I ask you to trust me as I lead you through it. I promise it'll be a powerful experience.

I start this chapter by sharing how, shortly after being saved, I was impacted by a film called *A Thief in the Night*, about the rapture and tribulation. Rather than filling me with delight, it filled me with dread. I go on to address how Christians have been fascinated by the end times since the first century and often struggle with how to feel about that topic. I argue that the book of Revelation is often misunderstood and therefore avoided, which pleases the enemy. The fact is, we are living in the last days or end times that Jesus and the New Testament writers talked about. In studying Revelation, we must remember that it references the Old Testament hundreds of times and says nothing that hasn't already been said in Scripture. This should encourage us. And rather than use current events to interpret Revelation, which we often do, I argue that we should let the Bible interpret the Bible. Based on the first verses of Revelation, we conclude that it was written by the apostle John to the churches in Asia. Like other New Testament letters, it wasn't written to us, but is for us. It is a prophecy meant to offer stability in challenging times. Though we often think of prophecy as telling the future, most prophets called people to obedience and offered warnings. This apocalyptic book gives an unveiling of our unique place in God's kingdom.

CHAPTER 2

THE GIFT OF COURAGE

Not long after my conversion, the church I was saved at showed the student ministry a film made in the 1970s called *A Thief in the Night*.[1] In the movie, all the Christians in the world disappear in the rapture, and seven years of brutal tribulation befalls everyone left behind on earth. It was terrifying. After the film was over, several students went down and prayed to receive Christ, but that night I had a hard time sleeping. Thinking about the return of Christ filled me with dread instead of delight, and that felt off.

The subject of the end times has fascinated each generation of Christians since the first century. Each one believed they were the generation to see the consummation of all things. What about you? When was the last time you thought about the return of Jesus and all things being made new? Have those thoughts invoked feelings of delight or dread?

The last several years have brought about a slew of questions about whether these are the last days prophesied in the New Testament. I have been asked: "Is the COVID-19 vaccine the mark of the beast?" "Is this politician the Antichrist, or should we expect someone who isn't an American?" "Was the pandemic the pale horse mentioned in Revelation 6?" "Are the recent wars in Ukraine and the Middle East significant in end-time prophecy?"

The book of Revelation is strange and beautiful, odd and awesome. It's frequently misquoted and misunderstood, and I think our enemy has his hand in that. To take Revelation from us is to take the crescendo of our faith and rob us of the hope that emboldens courage in difficulty. To misunderstand Revelation is to lose sight that God is sovereign over all human history and our victory is already won.

If the enemy can get you to avoid it or simply file it as too odd to understand, he can steal an understanding of how to live triumphantly over his schemes and plans. Before we dive in, I want to lay a few things out for you so you can see how I'm interpreting Revelation.[2]

The truth is, we're in the last days. When the Bible talks about the last days or end times, it doesn't have in view the last decade or so before the return of Jesus but something much longer.

Jesus interpreted the end-time vision found in Daniel 7 as being fulfilled in His ministry (Luke 20:18). In Acts 2:17–21, Peter preached that the "last days" prophesied by Joel have begun and that the "day of the Lord" (last judgment) has come in Jesus' death and resurrection. We see similar references in Hebrews 1:2, James 5:3, 1 Peter 1:20, and 1 John 2:18. It's apparent that the writers of the New Testament understood themselves as living in the "end times" or "last days."

The period between Christ's birth and His ultimate return has been called the church age. We are in this age. This age is what the Bible means by latter days or end times. What's my point? It's not new for Christians to feel and believe they're living in the last days.

LET THE BIBLE INTERPRET THE BIBLE

Revelation makes nearly five hundred references or allusions to the Old Testament, more than all the other New Testament books combined. Eugene Peterson went so far as to say that there is nothing said in the book of Revelation that hasn't already been said elsewhere in the Bible.[3]

This point is key as we seek to understand how God encourages us through the book. One of the critical mistakes I see is people trying to interpret Revelation through current events rather than following one of the primary rules of faithful biblical interpretation: letting the Bible interpret the Bible. In my lifetime, I've seen three or four supposed Antichrists, a few blood moons, a couple of alleged temple rebuilds, and enough natural disasters that I might have been written off as a fool had I tried to tie them to the prophecies in Revelation.

Pastor and theologian David Campbell helps us understand this in his excellent book *Mystery Explained*:

> The various plagues and judgments, for instance, which form a prominent part of the book, are to be understood in light of their meaning in the Exodus account from which they are largely borrowed. They symbolize God's judgments on the earth as these judgments are carried out from time to time in history: The woman of chapter 12 goes back to Genesis 37 and various texts in Isaiah and symbolizes the church through the ages. The woman of chapter 17, depicted as a prostitute, is to be understood in light of Isaiah, Jeremiah, and Ezekiel's portrayal of historical Babylon and refers to the wicked and fallen culture of the world and its institutions, which often form a demonic counterfeit to the church, thus explaining why the two women are described in similar but contrasting terms.[4]

A LETTER

Look at the simple sentence that begins Revelation 1:4: "John to the seven churches that are in Asia." Scholars almost unanimously agree that the book of Revelation was written by the apostle John around AD 90–96.

John was well known to the churches in Asia and used similar language in his gospel and other biblical letters as he did in Revelation: Jesus is the Word of God, the Lamb of God, and Living Water. This is important to understand because this book was written to a specific group of people in a particular place at a particular time. This truth should help you understand what God wants to say to you. He cannot say something to you here that He wasn't saying to them. Revelation was written *to* them but *for* you.

This is how we rightly interpret all the letters of the New Testament. For example, Galatians wasn't written *to* you; it was written *for* you. That's why I'm confident the COVID-19 vaccine wasn't the mark of the beast, and Apache helicopters aren't the locusts mentioned in Revelation 9:7.

The book of Revelation, like all Scripture, was given to the church across all time, not just to the last generation before the return of Christ. This simple truth will help us not take every new event in the Middle East or every new world leader labeled as tyrannical as evidence that we're the last generation before Christ's ultimate return. We may very well be, but I remind you that almost every generation has believed that of theirs.

We aren't in the same situation as our brothers and sisters to whom John wrote Revelation. They had endured nearly thirty years of increasingly violent hostility. It started with the Roman emperor Nero, who, in AD 65, launched the first wave of persecution against the Christian church that wasn't instigated by Jewish religious leaders. This was governmental persecution by the Roman Empire.

The church braced, rallied, and prayed, and they continued to serve the poor, walk in power, and share the gospel in the hopes that Nero's regime of terror would give way. Fortunately, it did; unfortunately, it passed to the next emperor, Vespasian, who used Christians as human torches, dipping them in oil and lighting them on fire. They were imprisoned. They were fed to animals. They were brutalized.

You and I aren't yet being persecuted in America and the West. We've had our preferences pressed on. I'm not saying that isn't significant. I'm not saying you don't need to speak up about it. What I'm saying is I don't think we should be quick to label every inconvenience or bias or ridicule as persecution. It's an assault on our preferences, maybe even an assault on certain liberties, but it isn't persecution in any biblical sense of the word.

In John's day, our ancient family was thinking, *When Vespasian is out, maybe it will get better.* AD 70 might have been the darkest year in Christian history for followers of Jesus Christ. In that year, not only was Jerusalem destroyed and the temple burned to the ground but some of the greatest hitters of the first-century church— Paul, Peter, and Timothy—were publicly executed. Imagine if, over the next year, our government pulled the three most prominent Christian leaders out of their churches, put them in prison, and then executed them. Can you imagine how disorienting that would be? How hard would it be not to live in constant fear for yourself and your family?

This brings us back to our church family in the AD 90s. They were following Jesus when Domitian became the next emperor and ordered all Roman citizens to worship him as a god. He set up a temple in Rome, and if you had the means, you were expected to travel to

Rome, go into Domitian's temple, throw a pinch of incense on the fire, and say, "Caesar is lord." He set up a series of laws, much of which involved the persecution of Christians. One such law was that if any Christian was brought under any charge in front of any tribunal, if that Christian wouldn't renounce their faith, they'd suffer the furthest extent of whatever punishment fit that specific crime.

When our Christian family in the first century said, "Jesus is Lord," they were making a countercultural statement. They were standing in stark opposition at that moment.

And now it's our turn.

The message of the book of Revelation is meant to bring stability in the most challenging times imaginable. It also brings strength and comfort to those subject to the usual temptations and minor sacrifices that following Jesus will bring.

When you feel the pull to withdraw, to check out, or to doubt your relevance at this moment, the Lord wants to flood your soul with courage and joy from on high through the book of Revelation.

A PROPHECY

Revelation 1:3 says, "Blessed is the one who reads aloud the words of *this prophecy*, and blessed are those who hear and who keep what is written in it, for the time is near."

When we see the word *prophecy*, most of us begin to think of future-telling. There are certainly examples of God giving insight about the future to certain prophets in the Bible, but by and large, it's not future-telling the prophets were doing. Instead, the prophets primarily called people to obedience based on God's sovereign reign and rule, and they warned the people what would happen if they didn't heed the call. Think of prophecy more as a declaration than a prediction. We see this in Isaiah, Jeremiah, Ezekiel, Hosea, and Joel, among others. Though there are some future-telling passages in these books of the Bible, their main message is "thus says the Lord."

In most cases, the people of God are shaken by the moral and social decline occurring in their day. You and I are witnessing this before our eyes as our present reality is hypersexualized, violent, and increasingly hostile to the picture of moral beauty we see in the Scriptures. Many Christians are afraid to say anything that might make them the target of an internet mob or create friction at work or in the neighborhood. (I'm not saying this is your role as much as I am highlighting what a prophet did.)

The prophets were God's voice to condemn the depravity of their day while calling people to repentance. In the Bible, prophetic literature calls for the people of God to walk in holiness and endurance, to reject the evil and rebellion of their day. Five times John, or an angel, called Revelation "the prophecy."

One of the primary things Revelation wants to do for you is call you to holiness and endurance despite the pull of a predominant culture that is rejecting and even mocking Jesus' reign and rule. Revelation is written to a specific group of people at a particular time and is prophetic in its purpose.

AN APOCALYPSE

Revelation is also apocalyptic, which is why it can seem so odd to us. Revelation 1:1 says, "The revelation of Jesus Christ, which God gave him to show to his servants the things that must soon take place."

The word *revelation* in Greek is *apokalupsis*. This is where we get our English word *apocalypse*. It simply means unveiling or disclosure. The purpose of the book of Revelation is to unveil to the churches in

Asia and us that things aren't what they seem or, at least, that they're *more* than they appear.

Apocalyptic literature, in particular, tries to do things that seem strange to us. We're not image-heavy people in regard to how we learn. We're fact-heavy people, which is why we struggle to grapple with the strange pictures and images in books like Revelation. Even John had to ask the angel showing him the images, "What is that?" or "Who are they?" In apocalyptic literature, people are often represented in the likenesses of animals, and historical events are represented in the form of natural phenomena, like earthquakes or floods. Colors and numbers have meanings. This means Revelation, like parts of Ezekiel, Daniel, Isaiah, Zechariah, and Joel, is full of imagery meant to inform our minds and ignite our spirits.

There's something imagery does to us as human beings because of how we're designed that's necessary for ultimate victory to be embraced. In this type of literature, the Scriptures want us to feel something as we know it. Pastor Darrell Johnson said this:

> Imagery has the power to hook us deep inside. Images can quickly and effectively convey what we struggle to put into words. Imagery goes beyond the intellect through the emotions into the imagination, grabbing hold of us at the deepest recesses of our being. Imagery goes beyond the intellect and through the emotions into the imagination, informing the intellect and igniting the emotions.[5]

Another reason God uses symbols and pictures in Revelation goes back to a rhythm we see throughout the Scriptures of God clearly making Himself known through teachings and commandments and then moving to pictures and symbols as judgment when people begin to scoff and mock. The symbols and pictures draw in believers while turning over scoffers and mockers to their folly.

In the Scriptures we often see God making visual displays that both draw in and harden. We see this in the book of Exodus when God made His desires clearly known to Pharaoh, who hardened his heart toward God and sought to be god himself. Despite multiple appeals from the Lord through the various plagues, Pharaoh wouldn't submit in worship and obedience to the Creator of the universe. His hardheartedness led to the Passover and God's victory over Pharaoh, his people, and his gods.

We see it again in Isaiah 6:9–10, which says:

> And he said, "Go, and say to this people:
> 'Keep on hearing, but do not understand;
> keep on seeing, but do not perceive.'
> Make the heart of this people dull,
> and their ears heavy,
> and blind their eyes;
> lest they see with their eyes,
> and hear with their ears,
> and understand with their hearts,
> and turn and be healed."

This may seem harsh to you and me, but in Isaiah 1, God clearly laid out the people's wickedness, and chapter 2 clearly warned the day of the Lord was coming. In chapter 3, God told the people in Judah and Jerusalem exactly why judgment was coming and gave them a chance to repent. In chapter 4, there's a reminder of God's commitment to making His people beautiful and glorious. And right before the verses we just saw in Isaiah 6, God reminded His people of His kindness to those who turned to Him, and He pronounced woe to those who scoffed and mocked.

Jesus took this same approach in His teaching. He often used imagery His followers would understand, such as the harvest, sheep, wine, and seeds. In Matthew 13, Jesus quoted Isaiah 6 and then increasingly taught in parables. As God revealed Himself through this imagery, believers were drawn in and sought to understand, while unbelievers continued in their scoffing and mocking. Symbols and imagery ignite curiosity and wonder in the hearts of believers. Those who mock and scoff at the clarity of the gospel will serve as a hardening agent, giving the person what they most desire: to be their own god.

The apostle John's admonition from Revelation 1:5–6 ties us back to what I have said so far: "To him who loves us and has freed us from our sins by his blood and made us a kingdom, priests to his God and Father, to him be glory and dominion forever and ever. Amen." The first thing we see in this passage is that Jesus loves you. Not the future version of you that has it all figured out and no longer struggles or doubts. You. Now. Jesus is committed to you. It's this love that moves us toward holiness and complete surrender.

Look at the victory He has won but gives to you: He "has freed [you] from [your] sins by his blood" (v. 5). All of your past, present, and future sins have been fully, freely, and forever forgiven by Jesus' blood. You aren't stuck in your sins. You've been set free from the bondage of sin and death and can walk in the freedom that belongs only to the children of God.

Verse 6 is what I'm trying to get you to embrace fully: He "made us a kingdom, priests to his God and Father, to him be glory and dominion forever and ever. Amen." John pulled this from Exodus 19, where God had freed the Israelites from slavery in Egypt and was establishing them as a people geographically right in the middle of the major powers of the day. In verse 6, God said to them, "You shall be to me a kingdom of priests and a holy nation."

Did you notice the subtle change of tense from Exodus 19:6 to Revelation 1:6? Look again. In Exodus 19, God used the future tense:

"you shall be." In Revelation 1, He used the present tense: we are currently. He made us a kingdom of priests today. Not the "we will be" of Exodus, but the here and now that Jesus has brought about in you and me. This was the first-century understanding of what it meant to follow Jesus.

The apostle Peter said the same thing in a slightly different way: "But you are a chosen race, a royal priesthood, a holy nation, a people for his own possession, that you may proclaim the excellencies of him who called you out of darkness into his marvelous light" (1 Peter 2:9). This has massive implications for your life.

Regardless of how you may *feel*, you belong to a kingdom of God's possession. This kingdom isn't limited to a geographic location, and the power of the kingdom isn't limited to certain borders. The power of the kingdom resides in you.

In J. R. R. Tolkien's *The Lord of the Rings: The Two Towers*, there is a scene that speaks to where we are in our journey together. In one scene, after the Battle of Helm's Deep had been raging and the evil Orcs and Uruk-hai had breached the outer defenses, it began to look like all was lost. Any capable males were given weapons and told to fight. At this point, Aragorn sees a young boy named Haleth the Son of Hama timidly holding an old, chipped, rusty sword. As Haleth hands the sword to the seasoned warrior, he says, "The men are saying we will not live out the night . . . they are saying it is hopeless." Aragorn swings the sword in an attacking motion through the air and then hands it back to Haleth, saying, "This is a good sword." Aragorn then leans in and whispers into his ear, "There is always hope."[6]

I wonder if you might feel a little like Haleth, surrounded by evil that seems to be prevailing, feeling not seasoned enough, equipped enough, or ready for what is happening.

Jesus, through the power of the Holy Spirit, is exercising His kingly rule through you. Not just through good preachers, authors, or blue check mark Christians. Through *you*. I wonder if you've seen this beautiful and glorious responsibility yet.

There are no spectators in God's kingdom. He has uniquely wired and uniquely placed you for His glory. As we will see, the Spirit of God will do a little checkup in Revelation 2–3 on where our hearts might be today.

As we examine Revelation 2–3, the letters to the churches could be considered a checkup for our spiritual health. Though we may fear the diagnosis, we can agree that checkups are important to reveal our health. The issues the churches faced in Revelation are the same issues churches have always faced and still do today. We must keep in mind that the letters address the health of the body of Christ, the church, not individual believers. We must also remember that regardless of what is happening, Jesus is present in it all. He wants His bride to be healed and whole. I then walk you through the letters to the churches, starting with Ephesus. They were doing many things right but had abandoned the love they had at first—their intimacy with Jesus. Laodicea's lukewarm indifference reflected that they had lost their zeal for Christ. They were no longer serious or intentional about their relationship with Him. While those churches had heart issues, others had mind issues. The letters to Pergamum, Thyatira, and Sardis addressed their double-mindedness. Though there was much to celebrate within each church, false teaching led them to doubt God's promises and compromise with the world. I urge you all to remember that we can face these same issues today and must be alert to the influences from both outside the church as well as inside. I conclude by sharing what spiritual health looks like in the churches of Smyrna and Philadelphia, offering courage and strength to endure.

CHAPTER 3

A QUICK CHECKUP

On Thanksgiving morning in 2009, I had a grand mal seizure that revealed a golf ball–size tumor in my right frontal lobe. After an eight-hour resection, we learned I had an anaplastic oligodendroglioma WHO grade III—or, in simpler terms, I had brain cancer. This led to six weeks of radiation with some low-dose chemotherapy followed by eighteen months of regular chemo. I've written about this extensively in other places, so I won't say much else except that God spared my life despite a prognosis of two to three years.

Now that I'm a cancer survivor, my annual checkups are more robust than most. Unfortunately, being radiated and poisoned can have long-term health effects, and my primary care physician isn't playing around when it comes to keeping an eye out for some of those dangers. Every year, I spend a couple of hours being prodded and poked and asked a ton of questions to ensure I'm healthy and to make certain none of the side effects of cancer treatment have surfaced in my body.

I'm not anxious about this annual tradition now, but I used to be. I've come to see these checkups as opportunities to evaluate my physical health and, if needed, as accountability to make necessary changes.

In Revelation 2–3, Jesus' letters to the churches are a similar evaluation of the state of our spiritual health. Through these letters, we get a thorough checkup of our spiritual lives, revealing whether we're spiritually healthy or carry some sickness in our souls. You might be tempted to avoid the scale to see if you put on any weight or put off that checkup with your doctor, but it's helpful to know how healthy we are or aren't. Do we need major surgery or spiritual medicine, or are we thriving? Do we need to change our diets or activity levels?

This is real life, not some game we can avoid or act as if it isn't happening. Our lives are fleeting, and we get to live only once, right? Yet we tend to minimize the value of our beating hearts.

This is spiritual war, and we are in it regardless of whether we want to be or not. We find ourselves in that same moment that Tolkien laid before us as Aragorn says to King Theoden, "Open war is upon you, whether you choose to risk it or not."[1] There is a battle going on—a war raging over the hearts of men—and your life is at stake.

THE SEVEN CHURCHES OF REVELATION

When the book of Revelation was written, there were far more than seven churches in Asia Minor. From the book of Acts, we know there were churches in Colossae, Lystra, and Miletus, but they aren't mentioned here. The letters to the *seven* churches mean letters to the complete church—the church everywhere, always. The number seven in Revelation symbolizes completeness.

Don't misunderstand me—these are real, historical congregations. But they also represent the church across history and geography. Interestingly, by the end of this chapter, you will recognize that the issues revealing health and vibrancy, or sickness and death, in the churches mentioned in Revelation are the same issues the church has always faced, including the ones we bump up against to this day.

I want to point out that these letters (which read more like royal edicts that would be sent into local municipalities to praise, warn, or both) are written to churches, not individuals. We can examine them and apply them to our lives, but don't lose sight that these passages were given to groups of people, to congregations. All the pronouns are plural. In Texas, we'd say the *you* and *yours* are *y'all* and *y'all's*.

What does this mean, and why does this matter? Well, as you are gauging your individual spiritual health, I also want to make the case that you belong to a local faith family, a church community where you're being encouraged and equipped in your calling. Knowing what health and vibrancy look like and what sickness and death look like prepares you to encourage and minister to others, and I know you want to be ready. But it isn't only about you and ensuring that you as an individual are your best, healthiest self. It's also for *us*, the body of Christ, so we can be a thriving, healthy church for each member and the community at large.

Notice what John saw in Revelation 1:12–13: "Then I turned to see the voice that was speaking to me, and on turning I saw seven golden lampstands, and in the midst of the lampstands one like a son of man, clothed with a long robe and with a golden sash around his chest." Whatever we find out about ourselves as we read this chapter, it's imperative to remember that Jesus is right in the middle of it all. He's not a long way off, not turning His face away from the ugliness of what we'll see together, but the Son of God is fully present in the very center.

I know John 3:16 is the famous verse, but John 3:17 has always led me to worship deeply: "For God did not send his Son into the world to condemn the world, but in order that the world might be saved through him." We see that idea here again in Revelation. Jesus wants the church to be healed and restored. He wants His bride to be beautiful and radiant.

And if you are a Christian, you are a part of the bride. He wants you to be vibrant, beautiful, and radiant. Maybe you aren't feeling that at all right now. Maybe you feel weak and ugly and flat or listless. It's okay. Jesus is here, right in the middle of it. So let's step on the scale, walk through this checkup, and see where we are.

EPHESUS: A BAD HEART

I think I won the lottery when it comes to fathers-in-law. His given name is Johnny Walker. He played college football, was in a rock band, and is one of the handier and most hardworking men I know. Johnny learned to surf growing up, and he has used surfing to help plant churches in Ecuador. He shows up to every event his grandbabies have, no matter how small, and has been a picture of what faithfulness over the long haul looks like.

Several years ago, by the grace of God, doctors learned that Johnny had several arteries blocked, and his life was in danger. He needed triple bypass surgery to save his life. Despite the fact that he looked fit and was extremely active, he was deathly sick below the surface. Without intervention, he wouldn't live long.

Similarly, we see in both the church at Ephesus (Revelation 2:1–7) and Laodicea (3:14–22) a sickness that we must be mindful of and order our lives in such a way that it doesn't overtake us. Although it looks a bit different in both places, it's the same disease: a genuine love relationship with Jesus was lost and replaced with something else.

Of course, none of us ever sets out to replace Jesus. But the enemy is crafty! Our spiritual sickness happens gradually over a period of time—a simple drift, a small deception, a tiny compromise, and suddenly we've turned away from the most important thing.

We know more about the church in Ephesus than we do about any other church mentioned in Revelation 2–3. We see the birth of this church in Acts 19. We have Paul's letter to the Ephesians. Timothy was leading in Ephesus when Paul wrote 1 and 2 Timothy. John wrote three letters to them as well. By all these accounts, the church at Ephesus looked like the ideal church. Jesus said to them:

> I know your works, your toil and your patient endurance, and how you cannot bear with those who are evil, but have tested those who call themselves apostles and are not, and found them to be false. I know you are enduring patiently and bearing up for my name's sake, and you have not grown weary. (Revelation 2:2–3)

The congregation at Ephesus had, in many ways, obeyed the letters written to them. Paul commanded them close to forty years earlier to be on guard because savage wolves would "come in among you . . . speaking twisted things, to draw away the disciples after them. Therefore be alert" (Acts 20:29–31).

The believers in Ephesus carefully and thoughtfully tested the spirits as John had exhorted them to do (1 John 4:1). They guarded the gospel as Paul, through Timothy, had exhorted them to do (2 Timothy 1:14). That sounds like a healthy church, doesn't it?

But in Revelation 2:4, Jesus took it further, like a nuclear bomb destroying all that was said before: "But I have this against you, that you have abandoned the love you had at first." Despite good doctrine, the ability to spot false teachers, a hatred for evil, and patient endurance, the church at Ephesus had a big problem—their affection and intimacy with Jesus had vanished.

Were they committed to orthodoxy? Yes! But their love for Jesus had dwindled. This was a really dangerous place to be. Remember, Jesus taught that the greatest commandment is to love the Lord your God with all your heart, with all your soul, and with all your mind (Matthew 22:37), so this wasn't a small deal. This was stage-IV, not-going-to-live-long news! It's terrifying. They were theologically thick but thin in love. They had good doctrine but bad devotion. This is devastating because Christ followers are to be known by our love (John 13:35)—our love for God and one another.

So let me ask you a deeply doctrinal question: Do you love Jesus? Your response is found both in your faith in Jesus and your experience of Him. Your attention and devotion answer it. It's one thing to say that you love Jesus as a Sunday school answer, but do you have a sincere affection for Him?

Imagine us sitting across from each other, and please hear the tone in my voice. I'm not scolding you or trying to guilt-trip you. I'm like your doctor, asking you direct questions because your health depends on it.

We love Jesus by faith, believing that He loved us first (1 John 4:19) and, while we were at our worst, Christ died for us (Romans 5:8). We believe by faith that God is for us and not against us and that nothing can separate us from His love (Romans 8:31–39) and that we didn't start this; He did, and He will finish it (Philippians 1:6). We believe that Jesus doesn't regret saving us, doesn't wish He could take a mulligan now that He sees us up close (Ephesians 1:3–6). We meditate on these truths and choose to believe them by faith. The Scriptures have been given to inform and stir our affections for Jesus, not as an end in themselves (John 5:39–40).

We see that our great enemy knows the Scriptures. He tempted Jesus with Scripture (Matthew 4), and the demons believe in God and shudder (James 2:19). What these same demons can't do is love Him, worship Him, and delight in His goodness and beauty.

David said in Psalm 27:4, "Gaze upon the beauty of the LORD." Do you gaze on His beauty? Of course, doctrine and biblical knowledge are important, but they should fuel our affection.

The church in Ephesus knew the right doctrine, could spot false teachers, and were enduring with great patience, but none of their actions were driven by love for Jesus. How tragic and devastating.

We love Jesus by faith, but we also love Him in experience—in those quiet moments when He tenderizes our hearts over the Scriptures or in a worship service or overwhelms us with compassion for a friend. Some Christians get a little nervous when we talk about experiences, but knowing and loving Christ is an experience. Our salvation is not just head knowledge, as the Bible testifies. That's why Paul, in Ephesians 3:14–19, prayed that we would experience Jesus' presence, experience His love, and experience His glory.

So let me ask you again: Do you love Him?

You might be in what some call the desert or the wilderness, and you aren't *feeling* much love right now. That's okay. I'd argue that sometimes love feels like desperation. We don't love God just for the feeling of love, but we love God for love's sake, even when the feeling of our love runs dry.

We see this in the Psalms on repeat. For example, David wrote in Psalm 42:

> As a deer pants for flowing streams,
> so pants my soul for you, O God.
> My soul thirsts for God,
> for the living God.

41

When shall I come and appear before God?

My tears have been my food

day and night,

while they say to me all the day long,

"Where is your God?" (vv. 1–3)

In this psalm, David wasn't being cute. He was desperate and long-ing to be with God. That's love.

There was no affection or desperation for God in Ephesus, and if we aren't careful, it could happen to us too.

LAODICEA: LUKEWARM INDIFFERENCE

In the church at Laodicea, their love hadn't been replaced with exter-nal religious activity; it had given way to indifference. Jesus said this to the Laodiceans: "I know your works: you are neither cold nor hot. Would that you were either cold or hot! So, because you are lukewarm, and neither hot nor cold, I will spit you out of my mouth" (Revelation 3:15–16).

This is a brutal pronouncement from Jesus. To be clear, Jesus wasn't saying that He would rather them be atheists than lukewarm Christians. In His message, He was using their geography as a lesson. Laodicea was situated between Hierapolis and Colossae. Each of those cities had water sources. Hierapolis had hot springs that were said to have healing properties, and Colossae had cold water that brought refreshment.

Laodicea had neither, so the city got access through a system of aqueducts. By the time the water got there, it was lukewarm and couldn't provide healing or refreshment. This is what Jesus had in view. A faith that provides no healing or refreshment and is just *there* makes Him sick. The believers in Laodicea had traded an intimate, loving relationship with Jesus for a respectful, private faith with no worship for fuel or zeal for God's heart.

What made matters worse in Laodicea was that they were completely blind to this fact. They believed they were rich, prosperous, and in need of nothing, but Jesus saw them differently. He said they were "wretched, pitiable, poor, blind, and naked" (v. 17). Their version of following Jesus was incompatible with what Jesus accepts.

I find mild approval to be the most consistent form of Christianity almost everywhere I look. This type of Christian gives lip service to Jesus. There might be a Bible verse on their social media profile, but they attend church only semiregularly and have little zeal for Him outside of a worship gathering or conference. They have no seriousness about holiness, little to no prayer life, and no love for His Word.

This passage says that makes Jesus sick. He won't be an add-on to your life. He is your life. He's not the top of your priority list, but the page your list is written on.

My guess is that some of you may see yourself in this part of our checkup, and it isn't easy to see. Look at how much of the gospel is in both these letters. Let's start with Laodicea since we just finished. Despite their indifference and ignorance, look at Jesus' response to the believers in Laodicea in Revelation 3:19–20: "Those whom I love, I reprove and discipline, so be zealous and repent. Behold, I stand at the door and knock. If anyone hears my voice and opens the door, I will come in to him and eat with him, and he with me."

Why is Jesus reproving and handing out discipline? Because He loves you! Do you see the invitation? The verbs *stand* and *knock* are in present tense, denoting ongoing action. He's knocking at the door of your life now.

Look at what He wants to do when you open the door: sit down and eat with you. In the first century, sitting down and eating wasn't the same as grabbing some Chick-fil-A. Eating a meal created a bond, shared life, and showed relationship. This is why the Pharisees grumbled at Jesus for eating with tax collectors and sinners. Here, Jesus is again knocking at the door, wanting to eat with those who are far from Him, have forgotten Him, or are using His name but with no real devotion to Him. He's knocking right now.

If you identify with this description of the church at Laodicea, maybe you should stop for a moment and ask Him to come back in to stir up affection in your heart toward Him. Confess that you have missed Him and want a love relationship with Him. This is what He instructed the Ephesians to do: "Remember therefore from where you have fallen; repent, and do the works you did at first" (2:5).

Remember and repent. Can you remember a time your affections for Jesus were ablaze with zeal? What was fueling those affections?

For years I've taught, preached, and written that Christians need to know what stirs their affections for Jesus. Yes, singing; yes, the Scriptures; yes, community; but what else? The Holy Spirit tends to meet me outside and in the quiet. My affections are stirred by early mornings and a great cup of coffee. And my heart will rejoice in the Lord when I can feast with a group of close friends.

What about you? What stirs your affections for Jesus? How can you fill your life with more of that?

We must answer another question as we remember those things that stir our affections. What robs you of your affections? These can be morally sinful or simply neutral things that rob your affection. I also think these things can be highly individualized. As for me, I can't watch too much TV. I don't think all TV is bad or sinful, although viewing some things can certainly be. It doesn't take long for me to laugh at things that break God's heart, and I give up my evenings for mindless consumption of questionable content. But I know people who are built differently than I am. They can engage with some of it in redemptive and helpful ways. I need to be more careful.

What about you? What robs you of your affections for Jesus? What distracts you from His beauty and majesty? How might you reorder your life to put in more of what stirs your affections and much less of what robs it?

The believers in Ephesus were also told to repent. To stop and turn around. Repentance is an invitation into the life Jesus has for you. What we see the Ephesians doing when the church was born was confessing and repenting (Acts 19:18). They dragged their sin into the light and turned from it, even going so far as to burn books of witchcraft (v. 19).

If you've lost love but have doctrine, or if you know what's true but are indifferent, then this is the medicine: remember and repent.

PERGAMUM, THYATIRA, AND SARDIS: DOUBLE-MINDED

If Ephesus and Laodicea had heart issues, our brothers and sisters in Pergamum (Revelation 2:12–17), Thyatira (2:18–28), and Sardis (3:1–6) had mind issues—specifically, double-mindedness. According to James 1:5–8, double-mindedness is doubting that God is good and will provide His children with what they need most. In each of these churches, and in our own hearts, there's a temptation to doubt that God is for us and is what we need. This leads to compromise with the world.

While there was much to rebuke in each city, there were also incredible things to celebrate. In Pergamum, they held fast to the name of Jesus and didn't deny the faith, even when a member of the congregation was murdered for his faith. In Thyatira, they were maturing in their faith. Their love, faith, service, and patient endurance had grown over the difficult years. The church in Sardis had a reputation of being a vibrant congregation.

As each church faced pressure from the outside world, they stood strong. This reveals that their double-mindedness wasn't coming from the outside world's influence—the predominantly pagan culture of their day—but from false teaching inside the church.

Our brothers and sisters in Pergamum who stood so strong against the outside world had no courage to challenge wickedness in their midst. Jesus accused them of tolerating the teachings of Balaam and Balak (a reference to Numbers 22–23) and the Nicolaitans. Basically, there were teachers in the church who didn't trust in God's goodness and provision. The pressure of the outside world, economically and in regard to the sexual ethic of their day, led them to teach contrary to the Scriptures, giving Christians permission to violate Jesus' clear teachings.

Our brothers and sisters in Thyatira were growing in their works of love, faith, service, and patient endurance. Still, they also tolerated "that woman Jezebel, who calls herself a prophetess and is teaching and seducing my servants to practice sexual immorality and to eat food sacrificed to idols" (Revelation 2:20). Like Pergamum, Thyatira tolerated false teaching around food sacrificed to idols and sexual immorality. These two issues would've created immense pressure for the believers in these cities.

Meals with food sacrificed to idols would have been common in the business world, where part of an animal would have been offered to the client's or business partner's favorite god, and the other part would be kept to feast gratefully to that god. This may seem harmless to you and me in the twenty-first century, but Paul had taught the churches that behind these images of wood and stone were principalities and powers—demons that were there to deceive and seduce men and women from the worship of the one true God. Therefore, to participate in these meals was to participate with demons (1 Corinthians 10:20).

Although promiscuity and sexualized images have been normalized in our culture, some of what passed for normal in the first century would make us blush or nauseous. For example, fertility temples were common in most major Roman cities. Prostitution of all kinds was not only legal but acceptable and normal.

By not participating in meals that included foods sacrificed to idols and not participating in the cultural norm of sexual self-indulgence, our brothers and sisters in the first century would have brought contempt on themselves and been treated as outsiders. The people Jesus described as Jezebel and the Balaamite-Nicolaitans hadn't denied Jesus. Instead, they were teaching a compromise. They were infecting the church with double-mindedness—likely teaching that what Jesus clearly taught, He didn't mean. They insinuated that Jesus wouldn't provide them with what they needed to live. Instead, they needed to compromise so they might be able to help others see and understand the beauty of the Christian life.

Our brothers and sisters in Sardis were stricken with a severe case of double-mindedness. More than a single teacher or group of teachers, the entire congregation was in the ICU with their doubt and disbelief. Jesus said to them: "I know your works. You have the reputation of being alive, but you are dead. Wake up, and strengthen what remains and is about to die, for I have not found your works complete in the sight of my God" (Revelation 3:1–2).

Sardis looked the part; there was religious activity in the church, but it was all for show. They had compromised and seemingly were no threat to the principalities and powers or broader culture. Sardis is the only one of the seven churches with no mention of hardship or hostility. They had acquiesced to the pressure of the culture and become harmless—or maybe *powerless* is a better word.

SPIRITUAL DARKNESS
AND FALSE TEACHERS

There are two things to consider as we evaluate our own health in light of these three churches. The first is that spiritual sickness and defeat don't always happen from the outside in. Sometimes they start in the church with bad teaching and weak discipleship. American philosopher, theologian, and pastor Francis Schaeffer famously said, "The central problem is always in the midst of the people of God, not in the circumstances surrounding them."[2] There will be a pull on us to compromise.

If I'm honest with you, I can consistently feel how odd I am in the prevailing culture. The pull on my heart to shrink back and be silent, to want to look normal or not offend, is extremely powerful. Even as I am typing this, I feel anxious. I don't want to needlessly offend, yet the God of the Bible will continually confront us. He is eternal; we are finite. He knows all things; we can't understand ourselves. He is outside space and time; our five senses hem us in a given location. This is a recipe for constant conflict if we won't approach the God of the Bible in humility. He is the Creator; I am the created. I won't always understand or like what I'm called to. But I love and am captivated by Jesus, so I long to follow Him wherever He leads.

The apostle Paul gave this warning to Timothy, who was in Ephesus: "The time is coming when people will not endure sound teaching, but having itching ears they will accumulate for themselves teachers to suit their own passions, and will turn away from listening to the truth and wander off into myths" (2 Timothy 4:3–4).

Unfortunately, over the last few years, there has been a sharp rise among churches today in those who, like the Balaamite-Nicolaitans and Jezebel in Thyatira, are teaching a compromise between what the world believes and what the Bible says about sexual immorality in the church. They seek to create compromise under the banner of Jesus' name, but Jesus isn't having it. To say what the Bible calls sin isn't sin. The sexual ethic the Scriptures continually set out as God's design for human flourishing is antiquated and obsolete and introduces the disease of double-mindedness. From this disease comes spiritual unhealth and eventually spiritual death.

The second thing to consider in these passages is that Jesus used strong language toward the false teachers. He said He will "war against them with the sword of my mouth" (Revelation 2:16). Referring to Jezebel, He said, "I will throw her onto a sickbed, and those who commit adultery with her I will throw into great tribulation, unless they repent of her works, and I will strike her children dead" (vv. 22–23). His critique of the church was that they were tolerant.

We live in a day where tolerance is viewed as supreme, yet the Bible doesn't exalt tolerance as a value in the church. In the Christian tradition, there are seven virtues that are pleasing to God: prudence, justice, temperance, fortitude, and the three theological virtues of faith, hope, and charity. Nowhere, ever, is tolerance mentioned as a virtue in Christian tradition or the Bible. For what is the first word of the gospel (Matthew 3:2)? What was the first word out of Jesus' mouth as He began His public ministry (Mark 1:15)? It is the word *repent*.

This isn't to say that those who struggle with sexual immorality aren't welcomed in the church as seekers. Jesus is saying we must not tolerate those who say that sin isn't sin and that God doesn't actually mean what He clearly says. It means we're serious about God's call to holy living and encouraging one another to walk in holiness. It means we refuse to believe the lie that compromise will somehow attract sinners to salvation and that we can be more appealing to the world if we soften those edges of our faith. It means we reject the demonic "that's just the way things are" of false teachers.

To be clear, I'm not talking about the nitpicking tribalism that's so common on social media today. I'm not talking about secondary issues. If you're wondering why the Bible puts so much weight on sexual morality, I'd argue that there's something mystical about sex. What we do with our bodies, we do to ourselves. The blessing and damage possible in our sexuality requires boundaries that, as David wrote in Psalm 16:6, "have fallen for me in pleasant places." To teach contrary to this and tolerate teaching contrary to this is to let falsehood enslave and destroy.

Remember, this is a spiritual checkup to see how we're doing. I'm not asking if you have any doubts or feel the pull of compromise. We live in a time where I assume you have at least moments where those flare. Instead, I want to ask you, Have you positioned yourself under strong biblical teaching? In the teaching you're under, is there an emphasis on the finished work of Jesus Christ—His life, death, and resurrection? Is there a call to live lives of holiness? Is sin or repentance ever mentioned? Is the teaching marked by the joy, gladness, and compassion we see in Jesus? Are you following teachers online or on your social media feed who are teaching a gospel of compromise with the world? Does your faith in Jesus and commitment to Him make you seem odd to those who don't know Him?

Jesus wants to confront the sickness of double-mindedness so that we might walk in freedom and not find ourselves enslaved.

The call in these three churches—Pergamum, Thyatira, and Sardis—was the same as in Ephesus and Laodicea: *repent and remember*. It's the call to those who are double-minded and those with bad hearts. It's the medicine that heals our sickness. Repent and remember.

- Repent by turning away from tolerating compromising teachers. Don't compromise God's clear commands to get along with the world.

- Remember what it was like to be alive in Christ, to be used powerfully by Him in your pursuit of holiness. Remember His promises and how faithful He has been to you.

SMYRNA AND PHILADELPHIA: A PICTURE OF HEALTH

Of the seven churches of Revelation, only Smyrna (2:8–11) and Philadelphia (3:7–12) were pictures of health. These two churches were healthy because of their deep love for, commitment to, and single-mindedness in following Jesus regardless of the cost. Jesus told Smyrna, "Do not fear what you are about to suffer" (2:10), and told Philadelphia, "I have set before you an open door, which no one is able to shut" (3:8). In other passages in the New Testament, an open door represents an opportunity to make much of Jesus (Acts 14:27; 1 Corinthians 16:9; Colossians 4:3). These two churches were the smallest mentioned in Revelation, yet they were used powerfully by God to make much of Jesus. I don't want you to miss the how. They did do this with their joy in the face of tribulation.

I hope one of the things that stands out as we have walked through these letters is that times of difficulty, suffering, and tribulation aren't things that happened only in the last couple of decades before Jesus returns. They mark the church age from the beginning—the coming of Jesus—to the end—His return and the consummation of all things.

This is hard to imagine if you live someplace like I do in Dallas, Texas. We've had an unprecedented couple hundred years of influence and favor. This hasn't been true everywhere, as our brothers and sisters in many other parts of the world have endured immense persecution and even death.

The Bible is clear: there will be tribulation. Jesus taught, "In the world you will have tribulation" (John 16:33), and Paul reminded us, "The sufferings of this present time are not worth comparing with the glory that is to be revealed to us" (Romans 8:18). The true gospel doesn't mean that if you give your life to Jesus, everything will go your way. Jesus isn't a genie in a bottle who makes your dreams come true. He isn't an errand boy who does your bidding. He is the King of kings and Lord of lords. We will gaze at the immensity, ferocity, and beauty of Jesus in the next chapter, but for now, Jesus is serious about your joy, spiritual safety, and fulfilling the days He made you for.

Smyrna's and Philadelphia's commitment to Jesus in the face of being marginalized, misunderstood, misrepresented, and even imprisoned and killed showed the world that Jesus isn't an add-on. Jesus is life.

This seems so counterintuitive in our current moment. Many believers today want to be seen as relevant or even cool, but God will reveal His glory in our joy in our tribulation.

Are you following Jesus in an attempt to use Him for some other purpose, or is Jesus the goal? In times of difficulty, frustration, or loss, do you come to Jesus with your hurt for comfort and grace, or do you run the other way, forgetting His faithfulness to you?

If you overcome—if you conquer—Jesus has made these promises to you:

- You will eat of the tree of life, which is in the paradise of God (Revelation 2:7).
- You will receive the crown of life and will not be hurt by the second death (vv. 10–11).
- You will be given some of the hidden manna, and He will give you a white stone with a new name written on the stone that no one knows except you (v. 17).
- You will be given authority over the nations, and you will rule

them with a rod of iron, as when earthen pots are broken in pieces, even as Jesus has received authority from the Father. You will be given the morning star (vv. 26–28).

- You will be clothed in white garments, and Jesus will never blot your name out of the Book of Life. Jesus will confess your name before the Father and before His angels (3:5).
- You will be made a pillar in the temple of God. Never shall you go out of it, and Jesus will write on you the name of God; the name of the city of God, the new Jerusalem, which comes down from God out of heaven; and Jesus' own new name (v. 12).
- You will get to sit with Jesus on His throne, as He also conquered and sat down with the Father on His throne (v. 21).

This is what the apostle Paul meant by our tribulations now being "light" and "momentary" (2 Corinthians 4:17). This is our future inheritance, and Jesus is right in the midst of it all—strengthening us, empowering us, and comforting us.

From here, Revelation pulls back the veil on everything we can see, hear, touch, taste, and smell and shows us ultimate reality, the epicenter of the universe. It will be a view that changes everything and will provide the courage and strength to endure whatever may come our way.

I begin by sharing about my preconversion experience with Christians and my confusion as they would go from casual chatting about the week to deep and transforming worship. However, I finally understood this experience when I became a Christian and started my own journey with Jesus. I argue that being an Overcomer involves seeing the ultimate reality for what it is. Revelation 4–5 gives us a glimpse into this other reality. John's vision begins with seeing a throne and Someone seated on it—the Lord God Almighty. This is important to remember. Even amid trouble and chaos, God is on His throne reigning. I then ask you to consider whether our worship is centered on the correct throne. It's easy to get caught up in life and place our focus on things that become idols. Jesus, who alone is worthy to unlock the scroll in John's vision, brings all things into focus. Although we think of this world as real, in truth, Revelation offers us a glimpse of the ultimate reality. Scripture shares many places where heaven and earth overlapped. Now, I argue, those places have become people. The Holy Spirit is present and active in us, filling us with power and understanding as we live in the ultimate reality.

CHAPTER 4

ULTIMATE REALITY

About a year before my conversion, the young man trying to introduce me to Jesus brought me to a Wednesday night youth gathering
called JAM, which stood for "Jesus and Me." I showed up to JAM at the
Family Life Center of First Baptist Church of Texas City, Texas. The
room was packed and energetic.

They started the night with a song called "J-O-Y." Maybe you
know it. "I've got joy down in my heart, deep, deep down in my heart."[1]
Then the guy leading worship called out "Spell it!" and the entire room
spelled out the word *joy* with their bodies like you would see a crowd
listening to "YMCA" by the Village People. It was easy to mock at the
time, and it was incredibly cheesy, but everyone in the room was really
into it. After that, they played a game, and the youth pastor came up
and made some announcements.

From that moment on, the atmosphere in the room shifted.

People's posture changed, and the singing changed. This was the early '90s, so they sang "Our God Is an Awesome God" by Rich Mullins and "I Love You, Lord" by Maranatha! Music. Before I knew it, these people who I just watched spell J-O-Y with their bodies had their eyes closed, and many had their hands raised, and it was like they weren't in the room with me anymore.

I accepted an invitation to youth camp later that year, and it just got weirder there. On top of singing with their eyes closed and their hands raised, some of them would get down on their knees, some would cry, and on several evenings half the room would pour toward the front of the room, crying, hugging, and praying together. Through all this, I was an observer of this place they would go. What was especially strange to me was that twenty minutes before this all started, I'd be talking with these people about football or a girl, and then all of a sudden, I was left there with the football and the girl, and they were in some other place.

I started to want to go with them, but I couldn't get there. I would try to mimic. I'd maybe close my eyes. I wanted to go, but I couldn't. About a year later, by the grace of God, the Spirit opened my eyes to the beauty of Jesus, and I became a Christian. When I became a Christian, I could finally go on this journey with them. I could leave where we were in the Family Life Center or sanctuary, and I could go with them.

A GLIMPSE OF ULTIMATE REALITY

In Revelation 4–5, we get to peer into what is most true in the universe. After the clear teaching of Revelation 1–3, the Spirit showed our brothers and sisters there in AD 96 and throughout the church age that there's more to reality than we can see with our five senses.

The Spirit wants to show you that too. To get to the deeper part of us, He'll use images and pictures meant to stir our souls and captivate our imaginations. A crucial part of being an Overcomer is seeing ultimate reality for what it is. Revelation 4–5 shows us what sits at the center of reality—the most real of reals.

The first image John sees is that of a throne (4:2). It's not just any throne; it's a throne that all attention and all affection in the universe is moving toward. There are twenty-four other thrones around this throne. Twelve thrones represent the twelve tribes of Israel. The other twelve thrones represent the twelve apostles. What's being shown to us? In the other thrones that surround *the* throne, we see God's activity among humankind throughout history (v. 4).

They aren't the only ones worshiping around this throne. Four strange living creatures are "full of eyes in front and behind" (v. 6). The four figures are designed to represent the whole created order of animate life, and their eyes represent God's sovereignty and faithfulness on earth.[2] Everything in human history and all of creation is moving toward this throne with attention and affection.

The most stunning part of the whole scene is that the throne isn't empty.

The last few years have made many feel like the universe is random and chaotic. I know it has felt like that to me. Trying to navigate the constant waves of tragedy, danger, and political turmoil while trying to serve my family in these anxious times, lead the church I pastor, and be a good friend has left me wondering, *What's next?* I can only imagine what things have been like for you.

In Revelation 4–5, God is trying to put new lenses on our tired eyes: there is Someone on the throne.

This person is said to have "the appearance of jasper and carnelian" (Revelation 4:3). The key phrase here is "appearance of." John was trying to help us understand what he was seeing. He told us the one on the throne is translucent and bright. You can see Him, but He's still somewhat concealed. There are vibrant colors and brilliant light. The one on the throne is radiant.

The one on the throne is magnificent and gleaming. We read in verse 8 that the one on the throne is "the Lord God Almighty." This title helps us make sense of some of the other images John saw. In verse 5, we read, "From the throne came flashes of lightning, and rumblings and peals of thunder." In Exodus 19:16, we see something very similar. The presence of God settled on Mount Sinai, and His presence was represented by "thunders and lightnings and a thick cloud on the mountain and a very loud trumpet blast."

His power is mixed in with the beauty and majesty of the one on the throne, and it is complete and terrifying. He is the Lord God Almighty. All might! He is all-powerful. Nothing can stay His hand. As the psalmist put it, "Our God is in the heavens; he does all that he pleases" (115:3).

If this image of God unnerves you, that's not a bad thing. The book of Proverbs says the fear of the Lord is the beginning of wisdom (1:7), leads to a hatred of evil (8:13), is the fountain of life (14:27), and inspires strong confidence (v. 26). This should be of great comfort to the men and women among the seven churches and us. God is on His throne, and He is reigning and ruling. God isn't blind to the pain, difficulty, and fear you and I endure in this fallen world. He isn't naive or indifferent.

In the right hand of God, who is seated on the throne, John saw a scroll (Revelation 5:1). The scroll's contents represent God's plan of salvation and judgment. The purpose of human history. Your story and mine. How to make sense of all the brokenness and pain we see and experience.

There's a problem, though. We see in verse 3 that "no one in heaven or on earth or under the earth was able to open the scroll or to look into it." This speaks to our inability to make sense of it all if we aren't gazing on this throne. When we look for answers, comfort, and strength around other thrones, we're bound to end up like John, who began to weep loudly because no one could open the meaning of it all (v. 4).

THE WRONG THRONES

A few summers ago, we were on a family vacation at the beach. Lauren set up on the shore with a chair, umbrella, and book, while the kids and I ran into the water to take advantage of some good-size waves. We had a few boogie boards and got some pretty epic rides in. Every ten to fifteen minutes, I'd look to the shore to find Lauren, only to be unable to find her. In just ten to fifteen minutes, the currents had swept us far enough down the shoreline that I'd completely lost sight of her.

This is what happens to all of us if we're not careful. The winds and waves of this fallen world will pull us along without us hardly feeling it, and we will look up and no longer be able to find where we started.

John Calvin famously said, "Man's nature, so to speak, is a perpetual factory of idols."[3] This means you and I are prone to set up our own little thrones and seek from them what only the one true throne can provide. Think of how destructive and painful this can be. How could the most common idols of self, others, and the world possibly strengthen us and comfort us at the deepest level of our being? They can give us momentary pleasure or escape, but each has betrayed us, failed us, and lied to us.

So much of our fear and anxiety comes from having our worship centered on the wrong throne. When I write the word *worship*, I'm not talking about simply singing, although that is a common expression of worship. I'm talking about attention! One theologian I know put it this way: "Worship is an act of attention to the living God who rules, speaks and reveals, creates and redeems, orders and blesses."[4]

My question for you, especially if you feel stuck or afraid or abandoned or forgotten, is this: Where is your attention? Where is your worship?

Fortunately for the apostle John and for us, one of the elders around *the* throne said to John, "Weep no more; behold, the Lion of the tribe of Judah, the Root of David, has *conquered,* so that he can open the scroll and its seven seals" (Revelation 5:5). John turned and saw "a Lamb standing, as though it had been slain" (v. 6). The Lion is the Lamb. Jesus is worthy to open the scroll and its seals.

Jesus unlocks the meaning of history. Jesus brings salvation and judgment to the world. Jesus administers mercy and justice, forgiveness and redemption. Jesus brings holiness and righteousness, wrath and peace. Jesus brings everything into focus.

That's why our eyes need to be fixed on Him and this throne. Why must we fight to focus our attention on His reign and rule over and above everything else? If not, we will drift. We'll gather around smaller, weaker thrones, and we'll despair, lose heart, and fade.

God has more for you, though. He sees you, loves you, hasn't abandoned you, and calls you back out to where the action is. You aren't meant to be a spectator in this great drama. That's what our enemy wants. He wants you to stay on the sideline, giving all your attention to your weakness or the strength of your enemies. He wants you to be afraid and quiet. And he's put a whipping on a lot of us lately.

In the past few years, many of us have fallen out of the rhythms that make us so dreadful to the enemy. We needed to retreat into our homes and attempt to be good neighbors despite the consistently inconsistent information around the pandemic. We couldn't gather with other believers in person, and new coping mechanisms became the norm for many of us. Our old compulsions or new ones flared. Where we thought we had victory over pornography, it reared its head again; that one glass of wine became three; we began to comfort ourselves with food; our screen time went up 900 percent a week; and our consumption of Netflix and Amazon Prime probably doubled. We're out of fighting shape and, if we're honest with ourselves, a little ashamed, or maybe we have simply grown comfortable on the sideline.

This isn't your destiny or your design, and around the throne, God is wooing us back into the fight, inviting us to come into His presence and return to the call of pushing back the darkness and establishing light.

God knows we are "prone to wander," as the old hymn says,[5] and He makes sure that, for all the ferocity that surrounds His throne, we know we are welcome and wanted there. In Revelation 4:3, we read that "around the throne was a rainbow that had the appearance of an emerald." This speaks to God's covenant-keeping nature. Not only is He all-powerful and doing whatever He pleases, but what pleases Him is keeping His promises. That makes a difference right here and right now. God is on His throne; He is all-powerful and keeps His word. The God who made us for this day and made this day for us can strengthen us, grow our skills and abilities, and go with us as we fulfill our destiny.

Eugene Peterson said of this scene: "All creation has come before this throne and is seen in its hidden beauty," which means it makes visible what you and I are unable to see in the natural.[6] Peterson went on to explain:

> In worship, every sign of life and every impulse to holiness, every bit of beauty and every spark of vitality—Hebrew patriarchs, Christian apostles, wild animals, domesticated livestock, human beings, soaring birds—are arranged around this throne center that pulses light,

showing each at its best, picking up all the colors of the spectrum to show off the glories. Around this throne, everything is seen as it rightly is. You, creation, around this throne is seen rightly as it is: beautiful and glorious.[7]

Revelation 4–5 shows us what's happening underneath everything that exists. The Spirit is showing every Christian across human history, including you and me right now, that this isn't a future reality but a present one. You and I aren't waiting to die to go there. This isn't harps and wings and sitting on a cloud. This is the ultimate reality, and we've been invited in right now. This throne room right now, these creatures right now, everything seen and unseen right now is in affection and attention pointed in this direction.

Several years ago, Lauren and I got sucked into the Netflix show *Stranger Things*. If you haven't seen it, some spoilers are coming— you've had years to watch. The show is set in the small town of Hawkins, Indiana. On the surface, everything looks normal. Families are having dinner, boys are playing games, and there's an idyllic and nostalgic vibe to the whole town. But as the story progresses, we learn of another world not far away. It's there in Hawkins, lying right on Hawkins itself. In the series, it's called the "Upside Down," and it's a place of darkness, evil creatures, and death. A portal has been opened, and the darkness from the Upside Down is invading Hawkins.

Something similar is happening right now where you live. The *major* difference is the world we see is the upside-down world with darkness all around. The one we're looking at in Revelation is the real one. When Jesus came, He opened the heavens and brought the kingdom into all our spaces. There's a portal open, and goodness, beauty, and light are pouring in.

That portal is you. You and I and all Christ followers are the place where goodness, beauty, and light emanate. That's why we need not shrink back or stay on the sidelines! The presence and power of Jesus is available to you at all times, and you are now an alien and a stranger in this present darkness.

WHERE HEAVEN AND EARTH OVERLAP

The Bible shows us physical spaces where heaven and earth overlap and intermingle throughout the Scriptures. After sin entered the cosmos and fractured God's design and shalom, God began to move toward His people. He moved toward them and revealed Himself through altars built and sacrifices made. We see it first through individuals.

In Genesis 8, the floodwaters receded, and Noah and his family exited to a world purged of violence and darkness. Noah built an altar to the Lord, and God met him, spoke to him, and promised that humankind would never be destroyed by flood again. God's presence, power, and voice invaded Mount Ararat, and heaven and earth met.

In Genesis 12, Abraham built an altar in Canaan, where God promised Abraham He would give his offspring the land and dwell with them. God's presence, power, and voice invaded Canaan, and heaven and earth met again. Throughout the book of Genesis, we continually see heaven invading earth this way.

After God freed the Israelites from slavery in Egypt, He commanded Moses to build a tabernacle so He could dwell among all His people (Exodus 25:8). This was a huge moment. God wasn't just meeting certain men in certain places—He would dwell with all His people. For the next forty years, God's people were led by God's presence and power and voice via a cloud by day and a pillar of fire at night flowing out from the tabernacle.

Heaven and earth overlapping and intermingling.

A portal opened to ultimate reality.

After the death of King David, his son Solomon built a temple in Jerusalem, and the presence of God filled it, and it became the place, the portal for heaven invading earth. Even in this moment, Solomon acknowledged that as beautiful and grand as the temple was, "the highest heaven cannot contain you; how much less this house that I have built!" (1 Kings 8:27). He was right. Ultimate reality across the entire universe is God's reign and rule from this throne we have been staring at. God's plan has always been to bring this reality into every corner and crevice of the cosmos.

In sending the Holy Spirit at Pentecost and His indwelling of believers, we see a new reality: these portals of God's reign and rule are no longer places but actual people. The Holy Spirit isn't an energy or a force. He's a person, and He is God. The Scriptures tell us He is the agent of creation and the source of illumination and power. The Holy Spirit is the presence and activity of God both in the church and our lives.

In some of the last few hours Jesus had with His disciples, He made them the promise that He wouldn't leave them as orphans but would be with them by the Spirit (John 14:18). That promise stands for us today.

New Testament scholar N. T. Wright correctly said, "Those in whom the Spirit comes to live are God's new Temple. They are, individually and corporately, places where heaven and earth meet."[8] If you're a Christian, then the Holy Spirit dwells inside you. He will lead you, strengthen you, empower you, and provide all you need when you need it.

What can man do to you? What should you be afraid of? You have all you need right at this moment to live boldly into your destiny. To live freely and joyfully into your identity as a child of God and your unique design for the days that God has made for you.

I know you can feel weak and like this is all too big for you, but you are a portal of God's presence, power, goodness, and beauty wherever you go. The Holy Spirit will fill you with greater power and clarity when you need it in a given moment. Don't wait until you feel like you're ready to live boldly or try and live courageously based on an emotional or spiritual high. Live by faith with your eyes on the throne and your confidence in the indwelling Spirit. He is God and cannot fail.

No matter where you are right now or what's coming your way in the weeks and months ahead, you are welcome at the throne that sits at the center of reality, where you are wanted and celebrated.

From that place of access to the throne, you're a portal pushing back darkness and establishing light. Whatever season we are in and whatever is coming for us in the days, weeks, and months that lie ahead, we must cling to these two truths. The whole world comes into clearer view when we do.

Although this life can be so beautiful, it can also be overwhelmingly difficult. We look around and see heartache and trouble all around us and experience much of it ourselves. As Overcomers, we are called to live courageously in this mess. Revelation 6 helps us understand some of that mess. We must remember that God is love. He is the creator of beauty and all things good and true. Suffering comes from the broken relationship that sin caused. However, I encourage you all by reminding you that evil and suffering have limits; they don't have the final say. God does. Though we may never fully understand the reason for our suffering, God promises that He works all things for good. I then examine the four horsemen in Revelation. The first is white, an imitation representing the false gospels that beckon for our attention. The second is red, representing war and the rage that leads to it. He stirs up anger in people's hearts. The next is black and brings famine. This one steals what we need for flourishing, leaving our souls famished. The final horse is pale, the color of sickness, something we have all been touched by. Though these horsemen are always riding, we can stand against them as we sing our songs to Christ in victory for what He has done.

CHAPTER 5

STRONGER THAN YOU THINK

On December 3, 2011, after I finished preaching the first of our two Saturday night services, I noticed a young woman who had grown up in the church. She was in town visiting her parents for the holidays. Lo had moved to New York, launched a successful career, and recently moved home to start a new initiative. We talked about life, faith, the church scene in New York City, and her plans. Finally, we agreed that we all needed to get together soon for dinner, and she headed out to look at Christmas lights with friends. I preached the second service and headed home.

Around 9:30 p.m. my phone rang, and I ignored the call. I'd preached twice, the week had been full of significant pastoral needs, and I was spent. Minutes later, my phone rang again, and this time I answered. The voice on the other line was frantic. It was Lo's mother, who was trying to explain to me that something terrible had happened to Lo and they were at the hospital in shock.

I'd known and loved Lo's parents for years, so I hopped in my truck and headed downtown to the hospital where they had taken Lo. I found out when I arrived that she had gone looking at Christmas lights from the air with some friends who owned a plane. After they landed, she stepped out of the plane and accidentally walked into the propeller, severing her left hand, slashing her head, and putting her life in serious peril. I walked into a room full of people in tears and disbelief and found her mom and hugged her. The two of us just stood there in the middle of that room and wept.

At the time, The Village was a young church, and all our hospital visits looked like this. There weren't too many seventy- or eighty-year-olds who had lived faithfully for decades and died of natural causes. The people in our church who were suffering from cancer were young—many of them children. The funerals were tragic and were almost always for twenty- and thirty-year-olds. The accidents were heartbreaking, and the caskets were small.

In addition to these tragedies and losses, people struggled with troubled marriages, addictions, depression, anxiety, and hundreds of other issues that were wreaking havoc in their souls. It seemed then, and it seems now, that you don't have to look very hard to find sorrow and sadness. Maybe you would add death and destruction to that sentence.

The truth is, we live in a fallen world, and it's a mess.

LIVING COURAGEOUSLY

If you and I are going to be Overcomers and live courageously in this mess, it'd be helpful to understand some of it. After we see ultimate reality in Revelation 4–5, in Revelation 6 we get more help seeing behind all the mess. We get some good news about how we can endure and stand with confidence in light of all this pain—the pain of others and our pain as well.

When it comes to suffering, we see several things in the Scriptures that form a paradox we should hold in tension as finite, created beings seeking to understand an infinite and eternal God. The first is that God is good (Mark 10:18), all the works of His hands are faithful and just (Psalm 111:7), and there is no darkness in Him at all (1 John 1:5). God *is* love. It's not something He has or does; it's who He is. God doesn't *do* evil; He does love.

Excluding Satan and demons who were made in the beginning good, it might be helpful for you to think of evil not as an action or a substance that flows from a source but rather the result of fractured relationships. It's first and foremost a broken relationship with our Creator, then with ourselves, with others, and ultimately with the world itself.

God isn't the creator of evil; he's the creator of beauty, goodness, and truth. Evil, suffering, and death are the result of sin and humankind's rebellion against their Creator, which fractured the cosmos. That isn't to say that every specific thing we endure is our fault. The cosmos is fractured at both the macro and micro levels. Some suffering, maybe most suffering, flows from this reality. The cosmos is broken. It isn't functioning as it was designed. We can know from the Scriptures that God isn't the author of evil but the source of beauty, goodness, and truth.

With that said, here comes the paradox: God—in His sovereign reign over all things—holds all evil on a leash, including Satan, demons, and the brokenness that leads to sin and suffering. Nothing, not even the brokenness of the cosmos, is without boundaries and limits. Evil and suffering are not omnipotent. They don't have the final say or authority. There's more in this part of our paradox, but we need to talk about judo to help us understand.

In the martial art of judo, the goal is to use the momentum and strength of your opponent against them. To use their energy and output to ultimately defeat them. Not only does God set boundaries and limits on evil and suffering, but He uses evil and suffering against evil and suffering.

For almost thirty years, I've watched as followers of Jesus have been diagnosed with illness, killed in tragic accidents, and on the receiving end of terrible tragedies. Yet, in almost every case, the peace that passes understanding (Philippians 4:7) does its work, and those people begin to minister to others who are hurting. Where evil tries to destroy, God turns it on its head. He sovereignly redeems the suffering of His people by exposing idols, growing their faith and dependence, and granting them His presence in unique and beautiful ways.

Here is our paradox: God is sovereign over all things. God is good. God isn't the author or cause of evil, yet when evil happens, regardless of cause, God can work things for our good and take the destructive hope of evil and redeem it.

I love this quote by Tim Keller:

Christianity teaches that, contra fatalism, suffering is overwhelming; contra Buddhism, suffering is real; contra karma, suffering is often unfair; but contra secularism, suffering is meaningful. There is a purpose to it, and if faced rightly, it can drive us like a nail deep into the love of God and into more stability and spiritual power than you can imagine.[1]

Having pastored for more than twenty years, I have hundreds of questions about what I've just written. I'm sure you do too. These questions can haunt me at times. The "where was God . . ." or "why would

God . . ." questions from people have felt almost too weighty for me to bear on more than one occasion. I don't just think of these massive questions theoretically and divorced from their humanity. These questions involve actual faces and real tears. The questions are cried or screamed or whimpered into the heavens. How are we to make sense of it all?

The Scriptures don't seem to be interested in answering all our questions. In the last five chapters of the book of Job, we see there are things we, as finite, created beings, won't be able to comprehend that God, in His infinite power and wisdom, can. He is good.

Look to Jesus. Watch Him as He reveals the kingdom of God. See His power over disease and death, His restoring power over tragedy and loss, His tears for the world's brokenness, and His power to do something about it. This is the kingdom expanding in every direction, whether we see it or not.

This is why darkness and pain are thrashing about. They're losing ground. They are trying to make one last stand in a cosmic war that has already been won.

THE FOUR HORSEMEN

I was ten years old when I watched Hulk Hogan drop his signature leg bomb on the Iron Sheik, winning the first-ever WWF championship. It didn't occur to me at all that I was watching theater. It looked real to me, and I desperately wanted to have "twenty-four-inch pythons" for biceps like Hulk Hogan.

One of the great alliances in the WWF was known as "The Four Horsemen." They were a team of some of the most colorful and gifted wrestlers in the WWF, led by the Nature Boy Ric Flair. They wreaked havoc on the rest of wrestling, racking up titles, starting fights with other alliances, and running things for years. The Four Horsemen were loved and feared.

This isn't the only place in pop culture the four horsemen of Revelation 6 show up. The Clint Eastwood movie *Pale Rider* points to the fourth horse and the one tied to pestilence that hades follows. Johnny Ringo quotes Revelation 6:7–8 at the beginning of the movie *Tombstone*, and there are countless other examples. There's something ominous but intriguing about the four riders in books, movies, music, comics, and video games. To stand boldly and overcome, we need to get a sense of who they are.

It's important to remember these horses aren't in some future event. This passage cannot mean to us what it didn't mean to our brothers and sisters in AD 96 or to all the Christians between them and us in history. Collectively, the four horsemen are the major players in the pain and suffering of the world. I also want you to keep in mind that Revelation doesn't say anything that hasn't already been said in the Scriptures. This passage follows the same order of Jesus' warnings in Matthew 24 about the last days that you and I are in.

WHAT A FAKE

The first rider is said to have a bow and crown, and he came out conquering and to conquer (Revelation 6:2). This rider and this horse—a white horse, white robe, crown, bow—looks almost identical to Jesus in Revelation 19: white horse, white robe, sword. But it's an imitation. It's not the real thing. This horse and rider wreak havoc by laying out false gospels both outside the church and heresies inside the church.

Our world is filled with all kinds of "little g" gospels if you're paying attention. They promise that this or that can save you, make you whole, give you purpose, and lead you to life to the full.

The most popular false gospel in our day is the gospel of self-actualization. This is the belief that you can find your meaning and purpose inside yourself. By finding the real you and living it out, you will be "saved." In this gospel, you must repent of the sin of letting any external authority define you. Not our parents, society, friends, and certainly not some ancient book filled with perceived contradictions and cruelty.

From there, the gospel of self-actualization tells you to go on a journey inward to find salvation. You look for your deepest desires, and once you find them, they become the foundation of your identity. Once you obtain salvation from external authorities and expectations and have identified your deepest desires, you seek a community of friends who will celebrate the "real you" as defined by your desires.

If there are still issues of loneliness, anxiety, or restlessness, you can add to your life any spirituality that fits your desires and the community you have formed. "Trust your heart. Go with your gut. No one else gets to define you. You get to decide your destiny, and you can have it all" are the creedal statements of this gospel, and it is everywhere. In almost every modern movie, show, song, and book, this is the gospel as the secular world sees it.

It's a false gospel, and you need only to look around to see it hasn't saved anyone. We aren't self-creating; we are created. We aren't self-defining; we are God-defined. This gospel puts unbearable pressure on people to create their reality in isolation while trying to make sense of the competing desires in their hearts. It isolates them and makes promises it has no power to keep. This is the white horse and rider: lies that say other gospels save.

Other pervasive, "little g" gospels are operating in our day. The gospel of health and wellness, the gospel of sexual identity, the gospel of social justice, and more. All lies, all false gospels, all the white horse and his lies.

Inside the church, it looks like heresy. If you're a Christian and have the internet, I'm sure you have heard all about false teachers and heretics. Unfortunately, most of it is nonsense and tied more to secondary issues than primary ones. Disagreeing with someone on a secondary issue isn't heresy, and calling everything heresy hides the very real danger of false teaching.

Heresy is teaching that erodes or goes against the core tenets of historic, orthodox Christianity. Think about teachings around the Trinity, how a person is saved, and the nature of who God is. If we think back to the letters to the churches in Revelation 3, this is more than likely referencing teaching in the church around compromise with the world—that you can love Jesus and have the sexual ethic of the world, or you can love Jesus and still participate in the feasts and festivals of the world.

ANGRY HEARTS

After the white horse and rider, we read, "When he opened the second seal, I heard the second living creature say, 'Come!' And out came another horse, bright red. Its rider was permitted to take peace from the earth, so that people should slay one another, and he was given a great sword" (Revelation 6:3–4).

The red horse of the Apocalypse is bloody and violent. The red horse and rider bring war. More than that, they bring the anger and rage that leads to war.

You and I, by nature, are born bent toward war. What we think about the red horse and its rider is what happens when rage and anger in the human spirit bubble over and get consensus and a nation rages against a nation in all-out bloody warfare: a terrible, awful scourge on humankind.

But what happens to the red horse when you *don't* see nations rise against nations? Is he no longer riding? No. He's riding—he's always riding. What ends up happening is in the background, for a season, he's taunting, aggravating, stirring up anger and rage in people's hearts.

I think this horse is trampling all over our culture. We are a culture given over to rage and anger as though it were normal.

In 2018, I read an article in *USA Today* about the growing trend of "rage rooms." Rage rooms are places where for around twenty or thirty dollars you can take a bat and smash things to pieces. We are a culture that has given ourselves over to anger.[2] We have all this rage, and we don't know what to do with it. You can take a bat and smash whatever you want, and you might feel better for a second or two, but that doesn't do anything to get that rage out of you.

Have you ever snapped at somebody you loved? It felt good in the moment, and then it's almost immediately followed by regret, shame, sorrow, and pain.

One of the heartbreaking things about the red horse and its rider is that anger and rage aren't primary emotions. Anger and rage grow out of sadness. Many people in the deepest part of their souls are heartbroken, yet they can't get to sadness or won't let themselves mourn or lament, so it comes out as anger, rage, and war.

Do you tend to fly into a rage? Do you tend to snap? What you feel under that is sadness or loss. Because we're so stunted as people, we can't access that hurt and wouldn't know what to do with it even if we could, so anger rules our lives. This is a significant issue, and the root is the red rider.

EMPTY BELLIES AND SOULS

As the white and red horse ride, we see the introduction of the black horse in Revelation 6:5–6: "When he opened the third seal, I heard the third living creature say, 'Come!' And I looked, and behold, a black horse! And its rider had a pair of scales in his hand. And I heard what seemed to be a voice in the midst of the four living creatures, saying, 'A quart of wheat for a denarius, and three quarts of barley for a denarius, and do not harm the oil and wine!'"

The black horse is famine. Like the red horse, we tend to think only of the ultimate outcome rather than how it roots itself in people's souls. The phrase "a quart of wheat for a denarius, and three quarts of barley for a denarius" is a kind of rationing of food that was poverty level. It was barely enough to get by. You would have just enough to eat and survive but not be full or healthy. The phrase "and do not harm the oil and wine!" is a command not to destroy the luxuries of life. What that means is this black horse and rider take from the world what people need for flourishing and leave for them the luxuries they don't need.

Is this not, in a very real way, a banner over the world in which you and I dwell? This quote from philosopher Elijah del Medigo captures our experience of the black horse and rider in the Western world: "The brutal, painful fact is this: the average person living in a Western country increasingly has nothing to live for. He has little family, few friends, no neighborhood, no community, and no God. He exists mostly as a ritual of economic activity, a number on a balance sheet."[3]

That's the rider and the black horse: nothing you need; all the luxury you want.

Little to no family, few real friends, no real community, certainly no Christ, just basically a cog in an economic engine. No wonder we're despairing. No wonder we're so prone to anxiety and fear. No wonder depression marks our world like it does.

The black rider has come, and our souls are famished.

THE COLOR OF SICKNESS

The fourth horse and rider are mentioned in Revelation 6:7–8: "When he opened the fourth seal, I heard the voice of the fourth living creature say, 'Come!' And I looked, and behold, a pale horse! And its rider's name was Death, and Hades followed him. And they were given authority over a fourth of the earth, to kill with sword and with famine and with pestilence and by wild beasts of the earth."

Notice that this horse and rider work specifically with the red and black horses to bring death to the earth—to kill with the sword (red horse) and famine (black horse). Pestilence is unique to the pale horse and rider, so he's aptly named the pale horse. The Greek word translated as "pale" here literally means yellowish green. If you've ever been around a seriously sick person, you know there's a color their body turns as it fights to survive. That's the color in view here.

They translate it "pale" because the fourth rider not only brings death; he brings pestilence. He brings disease unto death. Not only does the pale rider bring disease and death, but he brings it in such a way that it mocks our medical innovation. It mocks the sizes of our hospitals, and it mocks the breadth of our technology.

I hate cancer. What an insidious and awful disease. I've heard it called the emperor of maladies, and I get it. After I was diagnosed with brain cancer in 2009, I met several vibrant, brave, and beautiful souls who, like me, had been recently diagnosed. Each of us was really, really afraid, praying for greater faith, believing that God would heal us, and in braver moments, okay if He didn't heal us the way we hoped.

Over the past twelve years, I've attended or performed the funerals for those friends. In each case, I watched them waste away. As a pastor, I've watched former pro athletes, young moms, new husbands, and children destroyed by cancer and other diseases.

This isn't unique to me. You may be in the middle of treatment right now or have a loved one in the thick of the fight. I pray that the Holy Spirit would heal you or your loved one completely and miraculously.

The pale horse and rider are here, and death with him.

IT GETS WORSE BEFORE IT GETS BETTER

As if the four horsemen weren't bad enough, we have some extra ones here in the passage. You're like, "Really?" Yes. It's not just these four. It gets worse before it gets better.

In Revelation 6:9–11, we see a smattering of religious persecution. Then, on top of the four riders and religious persecution, we have just a dash of natural calamity in verses 12–17.

Why am I saying that those two are ancillary while the four riders are the major players? The four riders are true across human experience everywhere, always. They are always riding. They are always destroying. They're always bringing to bear what God told them to bring to bear on humankind. Religious persecution and natural calamities are bound to specific times and places.

The four riders combined with religious persecution and natural calamity gives us a grim and heartbreaking picture of life on earth. Look at the desperation in verses 15–17:

> Then the kings of the earth and the great ones and the generals and the rich and the powerful, and everyone, slave and free, hid themselves in the caves and among the rocks of the mountains, calling to the mountains and rocks, "Fall on us and hide us from the face of him who is seated on the throne, and from the wrath

of the Lamb, for the great day of their wrath has come, and who can stand?"

In light of the four riders, in light of the ancillary issues of religious persecution and natural calamity, who can stand? Who's going to make it? Who can save us? Who can deliver us from the four riders, from the ancillary sorrows of the world?

Can kings and governments? No. They're hiding in the mountains, crying and asking for mountains to fall on them.

What about those with great influence? What about our celebrities? Are they going to deliver us? No.

Our nation has a legit army with some sick technology. Is that going to cover our butts in the day of trouble? No. In fact, a lot actually plays into one or two of the horses. You don't beat war with war, spiritually speaking.

Is it the rich who are going to deliver us? No.

Everyone we look to for hope is huddled up in a mountain cave going, "What are we going to do?" They wish they could get deeper than the cave. Did you read it in the passage? They want the mountain to collapse on them.

And then the refrain in verse 17: "Who can stand?"

WHO CAN STAND?

The Bible answers the question "Who can stand?" in the first four verses of Revelation 7. What happens? The Lord—who has let loose these horses—has said now to the angels to withhold the pain and suffering of these horses until the children of God can be sealed, and then the attention turns to the 144,000. The number 144,000 is the number of completeness or a number of countlessness.

So I ask again: Who can stand? *We* can. You, me, and all our brothers and sisters in Christ. And we have.

After this I looked, and behold, a great multitude that no one could number, from every nation, from all tribes and peoples and languages, standing before the throne and before the Lamb, clothed in white robes, with palm branches in their hands, and crying out with a loud voice, "Salvation belongs to our God who sits on the throne, and to the Lamb!" And all the angels were standing around the throne and around the elders and the four living creatures, and they fell on their faces before the throne and worshiped God, saying, "Amen! Blessing and glory and wisdom and thanksgiving and honor and power and might be to our God forever and ever! Amen." (7:9–12)

I love this quote by Eugene Peterson:

These people are not only secure, they are exuberant. This is a curious but wholly biblical phenomenon: the most frightening representations of evil (Rev. 6) are set alongside extravagant praise (Rev. 7). Christians sing. They sing in the desert, they sing in the night, they sing in prison, they sing in the storm. . . . Any evil, no matter how fearsome, is exposed as weak and pedantic before such songs.[4]

So when the question is asked, "Who can stand in light of the four riders? Who can stand in the ancillary sorrows of religious persecution and natural calamities?" Jesus' answer is "My people can stand. And not only will they stand, but they'll sing in the face of the riders."

We can see this throughout our history. When the sorrows and brokenness of the world befall the people of God, we tend to sing. A great example from recent history is the spiritual songs sung by our African American brothers and sisters subjected to wicked and brutal slavery. One of my favorites is called "I'm Going to Sing All Along the Way":

> Oh, I'm going to sing, going to sing, going to sing all
>> along the way
> We'll shout over our sorrows and sing forevermore
> With Christ and all his army on that celestial shore.[5]

Did you hear it? "I will look evil in the face and I'll show it how weak it actually is." This is who gets to stand before God on the great day of trouble. *We* stand.

Why? Because the Spirit of the living God has sealed us.

HERE WE STAND

I don't want to soft-sell the tribulation and sorrow that's coming. These things are going to grow more fierce, not less, and we're going to see that in the years to come. But I want to explain it to you in a way that will root you in reality rather than a reality that would have you timid and afraid.

These riders have been unleashed on humankind, and we've steadily built anger and opposition. For what reason? Because the people of God are confronting evil all over the world, and the kingdom of God has spread despite their best shot. The four riders are getting frantically angry because we're taking ground.

I don't know where you are, but I'm in Dallas, Texas, worshiping Jesus. Here we stand.

What plague wiped out the church? What army knocked out the

church of Jesus Christ? What governments overpowered the church of Jesus Christ? What scheme, false doctrine, or terrible heresy has eradicated God's people?

Here we stand in the midst of a wild and discombobulating time, singing our songs to Christ. This is our victory, and the four horsemen know it. They know we're closer, so you should expect, like whomping a wasp nest, for them to fly around and want to sting, and even as they sting during our run through this gauntlet, we'll sing in their faces.

SING TO THE ONE ON THE THRONE

Around 11 p.m. on December 3, 2011, the initial tears had ceased. The wave of sorrow that would hit the room every time a new friend or family member showed up had settled down, and there were about twenty of us in a private waiting room waiting to hear whether sweet Lo would survive the night.

There were no words left when a family friend named Chris pulled out his phone, cranked up the volume as loud as it would go, and pressed play. The music and words from David Brymer's "Restoration" filled the small room, and all twenty of us—cried out, exhausted, and afraid—began to sing softly at first like a whimper, like a fragile hope.

As the song continued, the room grew in boldness, and the volume of our singing and confidence that God was on His throne and we could trust Him grew and brought comfort. But we weren't out of the woods. There was more bad news coming our way and some really good news. Lo not only survived the accident but has used it to comfort and serve others in Jesus' name.

While I researched and wrote this book, I could have told similar stories about Abram Drake or Charlie Dang, both little boys who died of pediatric cancer. In each case, the suffering and pain was unbearable to watch and confounding to try to understand the why and how of it all.

In both cases, these little boys and their loved ones—with tears streaming down their faces, snot running down their noses, and broken hearts with thousands of questions for the God of the Bible—lifted their fragile, quivering voices, stared the riders of the four horses in the face, and sang to the One on the throne.

Jesus knows that it might still be hard for us to understand all the pain, suffering, and death in the world and how to reconcile that with God being all-powerful, so He continues to peel back the curtain of reality to help us understand His grace and His just judgment.

I share that we often view Jesus as our "homeboy," a nonthreatening kind of guy. But while Scripture does describe Him as gentle and meek, He is also protective and capable of wrath. I then mention how *love* has become a junk-drawer word, meaning everything and therefore nothing. We love tacos, our spouse, and skiing. We've emptied love of meaning. Our culture further distorts its meaning, declaring that love includes complete tolerance. In truth, the more we love something, the more it brings about judgment and wrath. Since Jesus is love, His capacity for judgment and wrath are far beyond ours in righteousness and immensity. Revelation 8–11 offers a disturbing picture of judgment. But as Overcomers, we can see this as God's goodness and righteousness as we lament sin's grasp on the world. The seven trumpets reveal the corruption of nature, demon oppression, death, and unrepentance. This devastation is meant to lead people to repentance. I ask you to consider what we need to repent of and encourage you that God's grace is greater than our sin. Remember to pray—for salvation, through tragedy and sorrow, and for the world. As Overcomers, when we truly believe, we confess and repent, pray in confidence, and boldly proclaim the gospel. This makes a difference in a broken world.

CHAPTER 6

JUDGMENT AND GRACE

In May 2019, I was scheduled to teach through Psalm 23 for RightNow Media. It was designed to be six ten- to fifteen-minute sessions to be used in a small-group setting. The plan was to fly to Idaho and film the sessions in and around Sun Valley. In preparation to teach, I dove into everything I could about shepherds and sheep.

I'm not sure how I got there, but I stumbled onto myotonic or fainting goats. Video clips about these goats are hilarious because they lock up and faint when startled. Although the practice has fallen out of favor, ranchers used to place a couple of fainting goats among their herds so that when predators like coyotes, wolves, bears, or mountain lions attacked a defenseless herd, the fainting goats would fall over and be devoured, leaving the herd with time to escape.

When we filmed our sessions among the sheep in Idaho, there

were no fainting goats. There were, however, several Caucasian shepherd dogs. Caucasian shepherds are the largest and most powerful shepherding breeds, and they are quite terrifying. They've been known to get up to 220 pounds, and they've killed wolves and bears trying to attack the sheep. The shepherds working the herds in Idaho assured us the dogs weren't a danger to us, but it was clear they didn't like us there and would bark and bristle up at us.

I'm a dog guy, and although my impulse was to want to pet one of these massive animals, I put my hand out with a great deal of trepidation and reverence, walking slowly and cautiously toward them. In the end, I was able to pet the largest of them but never got entirely comfortable around its size, strength, and obvious power.

It's been my experience that many inside the church and those outside can tend to see Jesus as the fainting goat, not the Caucasian shepherd. For many, as one popular T-shirt says, "Jesus is my homeboy." The well-known painting of Jesus with white, feathered hair and a glowing face has reinforced the view of Jesus that removes His capacity for judgment and wrath from our consciousness. Jesus *is* gentle and meek. He does lay down His life for the sheep. But that's where His commonality with the fainting goat ceases.

The Jesus we will see in this chapter is much more like the Caucasian shepherd: protective, loving, and capable of wrath against those who would seek to prey on His sheep, distort His glory, and undermine His reign and rule.

THE JUNK DRAWER

In our kitchen, we have a drawer for our silverware, a drawer for pots and pans, and a drawer for bowls and containers. Then we have that one drawer we put everything else in. There's some twine, a vegetable peeler, a couple of random batteries, a few rubber bands, a meat thermometer, and some chopsticks. It's the drawer where we put things that don't have a specific place. Most people have this drawer. It's called the junk drawer.

Today the word *love* is a junk-drawer word. It means everything, so it means nothing. Think about how you use the word. Have you ever talked about your love of tacos, your dog, your car, or your hobby? What about your spouse, friends, or children? You don't mean the same thing, do you?

Of course not, but here's our problem: the word *love* has been emptied of its meaning.

To complicate things further, secular society tends to define *love* as complete agreement, support, and affirmation. To disagree or judge another is the ultimate sin in a society of supposed tolerance. I say "supposed" because tolerance seems available only to those who will completely agree, support, and affirm our culture's values. This belief harms those outside the church, and it erodes the confidence and courage of those inside the church because it's out of step with reality. Everyone suffers when we live in the confusion and absurdity of a make-believe world.

The truth is the more you love something, the more you tend to judge and the more capacity you have for wrath.

A judgeless, wrathless reality is one where there is no love. If you're a parent, you know this. How often are you judging what's good or bad for your child? Constantly, right? Almost all our yeses and nos are brought about by what we perceive as good for our children. That doesn't mean we hate our children; it means we love them.

What would you do to protect your child from someone trying to kill or destroy them? That would provoke the warrior in you; the mama bear would awaken, right? This wrath you feel isn't hatred; it's rooted in love.

Love makes us judge and gives us a capacity for wrath. We have the capacity to love others. Jesus *is* love. That means Jesus' capacity to love is infinitely more expansive than ours. Therefore, His judgment and wrath are right and immense.

In 1 John 4:9–10, we see this spelled out clearly for us. John wrote, "In this the love of God was made manifest among us, that God sent his only Son into the world, so that we might live through him. In this is love, not that we have loved God but that he loved us and sent his Son to be the propitiation for our sins."

Do you see it? Love has been made visible. The scandal of the incarnation is that the Son of God, the second person of the Trinity— eternal and omnipotent—took on flesh and walked among us. The love of God was made manifest among us. The active agent in creating everything we see and know came down and put on flesh—came as a baby.

This love is playing out among us! This love has come so that you and I can live through him:

- "In him was life, and the life was the light of men" (John 1:4).
- "The water that I will give him will become in him a spring of water welling up to eternal life" (4:14).
- "I came that they may have life and have it abundantly" (10:10).

This is love made visible. Jesus has come that you and I might walk in the light, have souls that burst forth with living water, and have life to the full. In 1 John, the apostle argued that we can't define love by looking at humanity, because all of our love is tainted by our sinfulness. All our definitions fall short. We have to start with God. He's untainted by sin and perfect in all His ways. This perfect love of God rooted in His character makes God ultimate in love but rightly capable of judgment and wrath.

However, this deals with only the first half of our 1 John text. Look again at verse 10: "In this is love, not that we have loved God but that he loved us and sent his Son to be the propitiation for our sins." *Propitiation* simply means the "turning away of anger by the offering of a gift."[1]

Whenever human beings turn their backs on God and elevate themselves to the role of God in their lives, devastating things happen to the person, to others, and to creation. Because God is love, God hates sin. Maybe you've heard the old adage "God hates the sin but loves the sinner." This might rustle you a bit, but the Bible says God actually hates the sin and the sinner.

Fourteen times in the first fifty psalms, we see God hates evildoers, and His wrath is on them. We see this in passages like Psalm 5:5–6: "The boastful shall not stand before your eyes; you hate all evildoers. You destroy those who speak lies; the LORD abhors the bloodthirsty and deceitful man." Or John 3:36, which says, "Whoever believes in the Son has eternal life; whoever does not obey the Son shall not see life, but the wrath of God remains on him."

Remember, though, God *is* love, which means He *has* wrath. I'm not trying to be provocative here. I want you to see why the gospel is such good news and why God's wrath is justified. The Scriptures tell us, "God shows his love for us in that while we were still sinners, Christ died for us" (Romans 5:8).

We see in Jesus that God so loved the world that He gave His only begotten Son (John 3:16), that Jesus has come into the world not to condemn the world but to save the world from condemnation (v. 17), and that Jesus came into the world to seek and save the lost (Luke 19:10).

Those who receive God's wrath choose it by siding with the enemy rather than surrendering to the lordship of Jesus. God has made a way for all of us to be saved and live life to the full.

THOSE WHO DWELL ON THE EARTH

Revelation 8–11 is filled with some of the more heartbreaking and terrifying images in all of literature, so before we dive into what's happening in them, I want to lay a foundation that will hold up under the disturbing and extraordinarily violent images that are meant to help us love the world we are in.

As Overcomers, we need to see God's justice and righteousness as a good thing while simultaneously lamenting the destruction sin causes in the world. The seven seals are how the church will experience the church age—the time between Jesus' birth and His return.

The seven trumpets that begin in Revelation 8 are how the unbelieving world will experience this same period of time. God employs the trumpets to unveil reality to those outside of Christ in hopes of getting their attention when all their idols fail to deliver them.

If that seems familiar to you, you're in good company with the first readers of Revelation who would have read this and thought about Egypt and the plagues, where God unveiled reality and used plagues to free His people. In Revelation 8:13, we read that the trumpets are the warning judgments for "those who dwell on the earth." This is a technical term for those who stand in the way of God's coming kingdom. It refers to those in rebellion against God and His ways.[2]

The judgments we read here aren't against everyone. Although we might—like Israel in Egypt—feel some of them too, we'll be protected from the worst of these judgments on the world. Starting with the fifth trumpet, we see that the locusts from the bottomless pit are told not to hurt those who "have the seal of God on their foreheads" (9:4).

In these chapters, God offers repentance to the unbeliever in the language we all seem to pay attention to the most: pain. He uses plagues to show people that all the things they trust in—their sense of self, peace, comfort, and meaning—and all the things that could be made and bought with their talents are blind, deaf, and lame idols that cannot save them. They're tied to demonic deceits that deform them from God's image, making them less than human. These idols and their powers gladly receive the worship of people who are made to worship God. Then they turn and destroy these people in the end.

TRUMPETS 1–4: NATURE GONE WILD

On January 6, 2021, A&E launched a new *Nature Gone Wild* series. In it, Greg Aiello looks at the destructive and bizarre ways that nature both interrupts and destroys humanity's desire to control it. It seems it doesn't make much of a difference what kinds of systems and structures we put in place. Nature breaks through them, reminding us that we are small and at its mercy.

We see this reality in the first four trumpets. Nature has gone berserk. Hail and fire mixed with blood burn up a third of the earth and its vegetation. A burning mountain is hurled into the sea, a third of all living things in the ocean die, and a third of all the ships on the seas are affected. The food supply chain takes a massive hit. Then a star falls from heaven and poisons a third of the water supply for all the earth, and then a third of the sun, moon, and stars go dark.

Now, for a world without a light bulb, without grocery pickup, and without a West Texas meat plant, their way of living has been severely hindered—hindered but not destroyed. Man is proven dependent and helpless quickly when the things he needs to survive physically are taken from him. David Campbell stated, "Through the suffering, deprivation, and death continually occurring in history, unbelievers are confronted with the reminder that the world and their lives remain in the hands of God, and their idolatrous trust in other things other than God has been gravely and fatally misplaced."[3]

Where the earth groans and writhes under the curse of sin, subjected to futility, waiting on the redemption of the sons of God (Romans 8:20–23), people die and are maimed. Villages, towns, and cities are rocked by earthquakes, flooded by tsunamis, burned to ash by fires, and starved in famines. In all of this loss, pain, and destruction, people do not repent.

Despite their idols of control and comfort being exposed, those who dwell on the earth double down on being their own gods and worshiping idols instead of the one true God. One of the ways you've probably watched this play out is in accusation against God. People reject the Creator God of the universe, decide to live their own way, put their hope in things that can't support their hope, and blame God when it goes bad.

What happens next is the stuff of nightmares. It's as if God gives humanity over to the ways of destruction they desire.

TRUMPET 5: A COMPLETE NIGHTMARE

The fifth trumpet is sobering and scary. An angel is given keys to the pit below the earth, which, when opened, billows with smoke; and out of it in the underworld come hellish creatures bent on absolute terror. They're led by one whose name means destruction and destroyer. The description of these beasts is incredibly detailed, and it has one main purpose: to describe a demonic power and suffering loosed on humanity.

Imagine your worst nightmare multiplied by the highest number you can think of, and you end up with these demonic beasts with scorpion tails. They drive mankind to the point of longing for death.

Do you trust in your body to save you? Are you pretty strong? It's not going to happen.

Trust your diet? Gone.

Your bunker and your canned goods? Gone.

Your stockpiled ammo? Gone.

Your social media presence? Gone.

The power of your stuff? Gone.

This is the world's experience with demonization. They are tormented and tortured.

As Overcomers, we aren't subject to this kind of torment because we've found our security in Jesus. We worship and pray, trust and repent, hope and lament, preach and fast. That doesn't mean that we can't experience certain levels of demonic oppression, just that the indwelling Holy Spirit saves us from the worst effects of these enemies of the world.

TRUMPET 6:
DEATH AND HARDNESS OF HEART

The sixth trumpet, the second to last of these calls to repent, comes with what would be the greatest death toll in all of human history. If you do the numbers, it's 2.6 billion people. The four angels are loosed from the borders of the land and lead an army dreamed of by tyrants. It's a horse-mounted cavalry of two million riders. At the time of writing, it would have been like the entire population of Rome with Russell Crowe coming for you.

A third of the population of mankind is killed. The description of these horses and their rider, if you read and try to imagine it, should show you that the judgment of God is serious, weighty, and merciful. A third of mankind is killed, leaving two-thirds the opportunity to humble themselves, turn from their idols, and worship the living God.

This brings us to what I think are the most heartbreaking verses in Revelation 9: "The rest of mankind, who were not killed by these plagues, did not repent of the works of their hands nor give up worshiping demons and idols of gold and silver and bronze and stone and wood, which cannot see or hear or walk, nor did they repent of their murders or their sorceries or their sexual immorality or their thefts" (vv. 20–21).

Two-thirds of mankind—having lived through the terrifying, restrained, and merciful judgment of God, having been offered life and deliverance, not just from a hurting conscience but from pain and suffering and death—doesn't repent. They don't turn. They don't humble themselves. They refuse to live in reality, and the text shows us why: because they're bound.

They're looking for purpose, meaning, and fulfillment in the things they can make or buy, offering themselves, made in the image of God, as worshipers to these things because they offer the most valuable thing they have: their attention. Unfortunately, in their idol worship, they give themselves over to demonic power, which has never actively stopped seeking to destroy those made in the image of God. These idols turn on their worshipers and destroy them, and these people become like what they worship: blind, deaf, and lame before the beauty of Christ.

You and I live right in the middle of all this death, brokenness, and despair. We were made for this day, and this day for us. As Christians how should we live in light of the seven trumpets?

Matthew 5:13–14 says that you are the salt of the earth—the light of the world. Amid all this catastrophic loss, we are examples of repentance. We are called to pray for the world and herald the good news wherever God has placed us.

After this next trumpet, the book of Revelation takes a three-chapter interlude before coming back to the seventh trumpet.

REPENTANCE

History tells us that on October 31, 1517, a young priest and scholar named Martin Luther nailed his famous Ninety-Five Theses to the door of the Castle Church in Wittenberg, Germany. The Ninety-Five Theses were demands for reformation in the Roman Catholic Church and would lead to what we know as the Protestant Reformation.

The first of the theses states, "When our Lord and Master Jesus Christ said, 'Repent,' he willed the entire life of believers to be one of repentance."[4] The devastation of the trumpets in Revelation is meant to lead "those who dwell on the earth" to repentance. We, as Overcomers, need to watch for any drifts away from total surrender to Jesus as Lord and King of our lives. If we are the salt and light we are meant to be, we must practice the ongoing ethics of confession and repentance.

What are you trusting in to bring you meaning and value? At that moment when you feel down, or you feel tired, or you feel lonely, what are you trusting in to bring you meaning and value that isn't God?

What idols do you think you own, but in the quiet moments, if you were honest with yourself, you realize you try to quit, and you can't quit? You delete the app. You put it away. You put the bottle down. You do *this*. You try to change, but you just can't change. You think you own these idols, but in reality, they own you. What are those things?

Is it how you're seen by others—wanting to be competent, successful, needed, enviable? You're working for what is already yours in Christ.

Is it whatever gives you control over your feelings—escaping or suppressing them? Like brownies or alcohol or sex or meds or drugs or exercise or another show or another thing you can buy? These are compulsions to give you a grip when things get hard. And they don't stay neutral. They take your attention and leave you thirsty for more because they aren't what they promise to be.

Or is it that our cultural discipleship has led you to doubt and disbelieve the reality of God's Word, His goodness, and the offer of mercy to you? Are you too sophisticated for the worldview of the Bible?

Where is it that you need to repent? God's grace is greater than our stumbles.

Jesus has grace for you. Jesus has granted spiritual power to you. Jesus has given you a community to trust. Jesus has given you His Word to cling to. The world needs Christians who hate their sin and can be the living embodiment of peace in calamity.

Overcomers are a stabilizing, unanxious presence amid moral decline and the world's chaos. Let's be people who continually throw ourselves on God's mercy in habitual confession and repentance.

PRAYER

In 2015, I posted to my Twitter account a call to pray for what was a growing list of police shootings. I didn't demonize the officers or the victims but tried to communicate that dark and evil spiritual powers were at play. I eventually deleted the post because it didn't take long for the accusations of wokeness or those who interpreted my tweet as unloving to minorities, twisting the tweet into something it never was.

What stood out to me was how many people with the terms *believer, Christian,* or *child of God* in their profiles pressed me that prayer wasn't enough, that it wouldn't ultimately accomplish much of anything. I understand the critique and believe that action should follow seasons of fasting and prayer. Although I'm not sure we are all that good at deep, abiding prayerful battle for the world.

Richard Lovelace put it like this:

> If all regenerate church members in Western Christendom were to intercede daily simply for the most obvious spiritual concerns visible in their homes, their workplaces, their local churches and denominations, their nations, and the world and the total mission of the body of Christ within it, the transformation which would result would be incalculable. Not only would God certainly change those situations in response to prayer—we have Christ's word that if we ask in his name, he will do more than we ask or think—but the church's comprehension of its task would attain an unprecedented sharpness of focus. Perhaps much of our prayer now should simply be for God to pour out such a spirit of prayer and supplication in the hearts of his people.[5]

As Overcomers, we pray. Through every tragedy and loss and death and sickness and sorrow, we pray. For unbelieving neighbors, coworkers, family members, and friends, we pray. We pray for physical, emotional, and spiritual healing. And we pray, first and foremost, for salvation. For eyes to be opened and idols exposed. We pray for our cities and nations. And we pray for the world. We understand what's happening in all the brokenness. The world will be judged, but there is a way out.

There's one more quote that has always oriented my heart to greater prayerfulness from E. M. Bounds, who said:

> What the Church needs to-day is not more machinery or better, not new organizations or more and novel methods, but men

[and women] whom the Holy Ghost can use—men of prayer, men mighty in prayer. The Holy Ghost does not flow through methods but through men. He does not come on machinery but on men. He does not anoint plans, but men—men of prayer.[6]

The greatest gift Overcomers can give a world under God's wrath is consistent, compassionate, and zealous prayer for salvation to come.

PROCLAMATION

It was after football practice, and I was taking off my pads when Jeff Faircloth approached me in the locker room. "I need to tell you about Jesus; when do you want to do that?"

His question disoriented me. We were in a locker room for goodness' sake. If you've ever spent any time in a high school locker room, you know they're rarely spaces of righteous conversation and honest dialogue about the meaning of life. Yet Jeff didn't care, and he didn't whisper but boldly approached me and told me he had to do this and gave me the option of when. I've never really gotten over that moment. His boldness and courage began discipling me long before I ultimately surrendered to Jesus as my Lord and Savior.

Jeff showed me the role of an Overcomer. He wasn't perfect and had a difficult life himself. Still, he continually threw himself on the mercy of Jesus, prayed his guts out, and then proclaimed goodness, mercy, and salvation to those far from the Creator God of the universe.

I was a mess: pretending to be what I wasn't, struggling with guilt and shame, and tormented by my own behavior yet unable to control myself. I was under the right and just wrath of God. He'd given me over to the life I demanded: a life without His reign and rule, without His demands and commands. He gave me what I wanted, and it was destroying me. When things got low or my mom dragged us to church, I blamed God for what I hated about my life.

As our paths crossed, Jeff quickly formed a relationship with me in which he wanted to share a way out. I had hundreds of questions and had a skeptical disposition, yet over time, the Holy Spirit started to soften my heart. Jeff simply answered my questions, invited me into his life, brought me to church with him, and prayed.

After more than a year of this, God opened my heart, and I believed. I still haven't recovered from the grace that "delivered [me] from the domain of darkness and transferred [me] to the kingdom of his beloved Son" (Colossians 1:13).

In Jesus' High Priestly Prayer in John 17, He prayed to the Father, "As you sent me into the world, so I have sent them into the world" (v. 18). Why did Jesus come into the world? According to the Scriptures, Jesus came to seek and save the lost and to save the world from condemnation. We are His heralds!

We embody confession and repentance, revealing humility and hope. We fervently pray, revealing our need for God's power and confidence in His work. Finally, we boldly proclaim the good news of the gospel, trusting that people will hear, repent, and be saved.

Can you see why it's such a big deal for us to believe—and I mean *really* believe—that we were made for this day? Why we can't shrink back? Why we must never simply be spectators?

God has turned "those who dwell on earth" over to their own desires. He has given them what they want, and it's destroying them.

To be an Overcomer is to embrace our calling to endure the brokenness of this world and let others know there's a way out. That God has made a way in Jesus for life to the full.

How are you feeling as we wrap up this chapter? I want to circle back around to something I said a couple of chapters ago. Jesus is the one enthroned behind the reality we see. He is kind, patient, loving and died on a cross so that humanity could be saved from the horrific pictures we see in this chapter. If we remove His just and right judgment and make Him more fainting goat than Caucasian shepherd, we actually diminish His perfect, beautiful love.

Overcomers are marked by love, and real love starts with total surrender to the God who *is* love and has made it visible in Jesus. His coming changed everything. When we think of Jesus' arrival, we tend to think of a manger and shepherds and a silent night, but we'll see in the next chapter, it was much different than that. Victory over all has come and has a name: Jesus.

I begin with sharing a sobering statement I heard about the Western church—that it is under a sort of satanic lullaby. We are often asleep and unaware instead of vigilant. Revelation 12 sounds an alarm to wake us up to the enemy's schemes. It offers two signs: a woman and the Dragon. The woman represents the people of God and gives birth to a Son, Jesus Christ. The Dragon is Satan, a murderer and deceiver. There is enmity and war between the two. Unfortunately, we are often asleep to the reality that a cosmic war is going on around us. We are in spiritual danger from an enemy who wants to destroy us. When we are sleeping, we are easy to destroy. However, as Overcomers, we become a threat to the enemy. I share that the enemy started accusing me when I was a child, and I imagine that is the case with many people. Satan gets us to believe his lies and uses our wounds against us. He not only accuses but deceives. He convinces us as individuals to believe things about God that aren't true and also attacks the church. However, as children of the King, we are a powerful weapon against the enemy and his dark forces. But we must be alert.

CHAPTER 7

VICTORY IS HERE

My wife is a singer and songwriter—an incredible gift to my family as our house has always been full of music and song. When our kids were younger, I'd often hear Lauren upstairs sweetly singing the promises of God over them while she scratched their backs softly or played with their hair. Those lullabies would calm their souls and usher them into a deep and satisfying sleep regardless of how the day went for them.

If they woke up with a nightmare, they'd come to her side of the bed, and the beauty of the lullaby would flow from Lauren's lungs and vocal folds, and the fear would melt away to be replaced with peace. Before long, they'd be back in their beds, sleeping soundly. I love the memories of my wife calming, healing, and allowing peace to flow through her and onto our babies.

In some of my dark moments, she would sing over me. It was not uncommon for her to hum or sing as I endured chemotherapy during my battle with brain cancer.

In March 2020, Lauren and I were invited to attend the IF: Gathering, which was founded by our dear friend Jennie Allen. We've been in the IF family since its inception, and one of the sessions that year was Jennie interviewing a pastor who led a massive underground house church movement in Iran. There are a lot of reports coming out of the Middle East that Iran is in the middle of a large-scale revival, with tens of thousands of Iranians coming to know Jesus. Through dreams, visions, and other miraculous means, the good news of Jesus is overcoming a tyrannical and violent regime—like it did in Rome, like it did in the Ottoman Empire, like it did in the USSR, like it is doing in China and other nations around the world. His story deeply moved me.[1]

In the interview, Jennie asked this pastor about his perception of the Western church. Normally, when people talk about the "West" or the "Western church," I raise an eyebrow. I know we aren't perfect and have a lot of work to do, but harshly critiquing the West without at least a nod to some of the beautiful and good the West has brought into the world has always felt disingenuous to me.

The pastor responded with a quote from his wife that deeply resonated with me and has haunted me since I heard him say it.

Without any guile or judgment, he said, "It seems to me that the church in the West is under some sort of satanic lullaby." He went on to describe us as asleep and unaware of what we're caught up in. He highlighted several ways that he noticed we were asleep. As a pastor in the Bible Belt of the West, I couldn't disagree with his assessment.

That's not to say there aren't some of us who are completely awake and right in the middle of it all, but he was right. We're asleep.

A lullaby is a beautiful gift when it's time to sleep and is a monstrous melody when it's time to be vigilant and wide awake. Revelation

12 is the alarm we need. In this provoking and powerful chapter, we get two signs and the schemes of our enemy. It's a picture of the cosmic war you and I are caught up in and a call to be wide awake against the enemy, who is thrashing about.

THE WOMAN

The first sign we're given is one of a woman. If we were to draw her, she'd look exceptionally odd. She is clothed with the sun, with the moon under her feet, and on her head she's wearing a crown with twelve stars (12:1). Verse 2 tells us she's pregnant and cries out in birth pains and the agony of giving birth. A straight reading of this chapter leads us to believe this is Mary, and I believe it is, but I think it is bigger than just Mary. I say that because of the sun, moon, and stars in the passage.

Remember, everything in Revelation has already been said in the Bible. In Genesis 37:9, Joseph dreamed of the sun, moon, and eleven stars bowing to him. The sun is his father, Jacob; the moon is his mother, Rachel; and the eleven stars are his brothers, with Joseph being the twelfth star. In Revelation 12, this sign of a woman with the twelve stars in her crown is Israel, the people of God.

The prophet Isaiah said there's coming a time when the people of God will give birth to one who will make war against the Dragon. Isaiah 66:7–9 says this:

> "Before she was in labor
> she gave birth;
> before her pain came upon her
> she delivered a son.
> Who has heard such a thing?

Who has seen such things?

Shall a land be born in one day?

Shall a nation be brought forth in one moment?

For as soon as Zion was in labor

she brought forth her children.

Shall I bring to the point of birth and not cause to bring forth?"

says the LORD;

"shall I, who cause to bring forth, shut the womb?"

says your God.

The prophet Isaiah was saying the people of God would give birth to the one who would make war against the Dragon. So the woman is a sign of the people of God, both before Jesus and after Jesus. She represents Israel, Mary, and the church all at once. She is the ideal church as she's seen in heaven.

She's not the only sign, though. In verses 3–6 and verse 9, John is shown another sign.

THE DRAGON

In verse 9, we see who the Dragon is in verse 3. Revelation 12:9 says, "And the great dragon was thrown down, that ancient serpent, who is called the devil and Satan, the deceiver of the whole world—he was thrown down to the earth, and his angels were thrown down with him."

His color is red, the color of blood. He is a killer. He is a murderer. He is violent. He has seven heads, representing complete authority, albeit borrowed authority. Not ultimately *his* authority, the authority given to him by God. He has ten horns. Horns are a symbol of strength. Ten is a lot of strength.

In Genesis 3:15, we see that there will be enmity between the woman and the serpent and a coming collision where an offspring of the woman will bruise the head of the serpent, and the serpent will bruise His heel. There's war and enmity between the Dragon and the people of God.

One of the things that happens historically and consistently when a culture gives itself over to depravity and wickedness—when a culture turns its back on the things of God—is that women and children suffer the most.

Scholar Stephen Dempster said one of the great themes of the Old Testament is woman against beast:

Eve versus the serpent; Sarah and Rebekah versus barrenness; Tamar versus Judah; Jochebed and Miriam versus the Pharaoh; Deborah and Jael versus Sisera; Ruth and Naomi versus death; Hannah versus barrenness; Jehosheba versus Athaliah. In all these examples of struggle, these women of faith are engaged in a battle to save the people of God. The victory of Esther over Haman dramatically continues this theme.[2]

Ladies, Satan hates you. Men, Satan hates your sisters, wives, and daughters. He wants to destroy women. He wants to devour our children. This is what we need to wake up to.

This isn't a passage full of bad news. Look at Revelation 12:5–6: "She gave birth to a male child, one who is to rule all the nations with a rod of iron, but her child was caught up to God and to his throne, and the woman fled into the wilderness, where she has a place prepared by God, in which she is to be nourished for 1,260 days."

The woman gave birth to a Son. The Son is not a sign. The Son will rule with an iron scepter. The Son is Jesus Christ. In Matthew 2, Mary gave birth to Jesus, and we read about Herod setting his face to kill every boy under the age of two (v. 16). This is the Dragon getting ready to pounce on the Son. When the angel appeared to Joseph and told them to flee to Egypt, they went to the place prepared by God.

This is a very different Christmas story than the one we usually read in December, isn't it? We're used to the silent, holy night told in the Gospels, and that's true and beautiful.

But behind all that in the cosmos, there's war between the Dragon and the people of God. It might have been calm and bright on the surface, but behind what was visible to human beings, there were clashes between principalities and powers that would make our world wars look like mere skirmishes.

THE SCHEMES

We are asleep to the people of God versus the Dragon and the Dragon versus the people of God. When was the last time you were awake, and I mean wide awake, to the reality that you're caught up in a cosmic war? Do you ever feel that you're in spiritual danger? That you have an enemy who wants to destroy you?

I wonder if how we think about church, our home group or Sunday school class, holiness and prayer, and the Bible reveals that we believe we're in some sort of all-inclusive Caribbean paradise where Jesus is going to bring us the tropical beverages of choice. Or do we realize we're in danger and have an ancient evil hunting and harassing us?

A sleeping enemy is an easy enemy to destroy. That's why this chapter is so important. As Overcomers, we have to be aware that we have a real enemy, and he plans to kill, steal, and destroy us (John 10:10). The beautiful thing about Revelation 12 is that we see the Dragon and how he fights. If we wake up to the Dragon and how the

Dragon fights, he loses his power, and we become more problematic to him than we can fathom.

You are an Overcomer, a major problem to him.

He hates you, but he can't do much about it once you know his plan of attack. He wants to accuse you, deceive you, and cause you to fear death. If he can do that, he can take you completely out of the game. He can keep you asleep.

If you wake up and see him for what he is, it's over. You will wake up and bring light, life, and order to the places God has planted you.

ACCUSATION

As I mentioned, I was around six years old when I remember seeing a counselor for the first time. It wasn't just me; it was my entire family. I didn't know at the time why we were there. My parents may have explained it to me, but I have no memory of that. I took from those counseling sessions that something was wrong with me that was causing our family not to work, that I was broken and couldn't be trusted.

My counselor didn't say that to me. My parents didn't say that to me. My sisters didn't say that to me, yet this is how I interpreted the entire affair. For years, the lies that I ruin things, that something was deeply wrong with me, and that I couldn't be trusted grew up with me as I physically grew.

I was not aware that I was having those thoughts. It was happening deep under the surface, stealing my capacity to receive love from others, killing my ability to trust that God delights in me, and destroying any chance to live out of the joy of being fully known yet fully loved. It would take a whole book to explain the havoc these lies wreaked on my life. The self-hate, the stealing of confidence, the passivity and fear were sown into the deepest part of me. It was the

Dragon, and he started when I was six. My guess is he started on you pretty early too. This is one of his primary strategies—to accuse us. To get us to believe lies.

In Revelation 12:10, we read, "And I heard a loud voice in heaven, saying, 'Now the salvation and the power and the kingdom of our God and the authority of his Christ have come, for the accuser of our brothers has been thrown down, who accuses them day and night before our God.'"

The Dragon accuses us and then accuses us before God. We covered this in the introduction, but Satan usually uses words or wounds to start the accusations. In my case, the purpose of our family counseling had nothing to do with me, yet he took advantage of the situation and sowed lies into my spirit that grew up with me in ways that were impossible for me to spot.

It might be something that was said or done to you that the Dragon used as a way to lie, to accuse, and to sing you to sleep so you would be unaware of the war and unaware of how powerful you can be. His goal is simple: keep you away from the power and presence of Jesus.

If the enemy can hassle you to the point that you believe God cannot love you because of your sin or cause you to despise others, he'll cut you off from the power to wage war against him and rob you of the glory and joy of walking in victory. If he can get you to doubt God's love and delight in you, you'll run from God rather than abide in His presence. You will neglect the Scriptures, which are the sword of the Spirit (Ephesians 6:17), and you won't labor in prayer, which accomplishes more against the enemy than we can imagine. This is his primary tactic, and we're oblivious to it.

Let me give you some simple and common examples. Recently, a young woman was baptized at the church I pastor. As she tearfully shared her testimony, she told a room full of people that she had an abortion when she was in college, leading to a tremendous amount of guilt and shame. Over the years, many friends had shared the gospel with her, prayed for her, and sought to love her well. That morning, she confessed that each time she heard the gospel, she thought, *Except for someone like me.*

Do you see what happened? Despite the fact that most of the heroes of the Bible couldn't pass a background check, this woman believed she had outsinned the grace of God. Where did she get that? The Bible says, "Where sin increased, grace abounded all the more" (Romans 5:20). So it's not from what the Bible teaches. It's the Dragon, the Accuser, Satan, trying to keep her asleep.

That day as she shared her darkest secret, the men and women of The Village Church gave her a standing ovation. They were praising God for His victory over the accusations of the enemy. The transferring of this beautiful young woman out of the domain of darkness and into the kingdom of His beloved Son. Since waking up, she's been a force. She's serving other women caught in shame and self-hatred, walking in contagious joy, and enjoying the love of Jesus and others more deeply than she thought possible.

I'm seeking to wake you up to the fact that you're no ordinary soul. You are a child of the King, a weapon against the forces of darkness—a significant force.

I wonder if you have a hard time believing it because, like the story above, you have a moment—maybe even moments—in your life that the Accuser uses to haunt you or a present struggle that makes you feel paralyzed. Like the woman above, you have been reading these pages and thinking, *Except for someone like me.*

I hope you can see what's happening. Please hear me, friend; you cannot outsin the grace of God. Jesus knew what He was buying on the cross—you! Not the future version of you that you think will be all clean and tidy. You *now.*

He loved you "before the foundation of the world" (Ephesians 1:4).

He knows your past and sees everything in your present and still calls you child, and in John 15:14, He calls you friend! He won't quit you or give up on you.

If you're currently struggling with secret sin or feel stuck in shame, don't let the enemy take from you what Jesus died to give you—namely, intimacy with Him through the Spirit. You're on a lifelong journey of becoming more and more like Jesus. He's aware of the time it takes to heal and shape you. Take your fears and hurts to Him, confess your sins, and get some help. You might not have a congregation give you a standing ovation like the woman in the story above, but you will get the applause of heaven, pictured in Jesus' parables in Luke 15!

Jesus is on your side. I hope your heart is softening, and I hope you can almost hear the cheers of heaven and the shudder of fear down the back of your enemy.

In my twenty years of pastoral ministry, I've watched hundreds and hundreds of people robbed of the joy of intimacy with Jesus by some silly accusations from the enemy. I'd be failing in my pastoral duties if I didn't try to shine a light on the two most common accusations.

"YOU'RE NOT GOOD AT PRAYER"

One of the more frequent things Christians will say to me is that they don't know how to pray.

I usually ask a few follow-up questions. "What do you mean? Are you saying you don't pray as long as you want? Are you saying that you don't think you are praying with as much power as you believe you should be praying with? What specifically do you mean?"

Almost everyone I know, including me, would love to pray longer and with more power. I'm consistently shocked by how many have convinced themselves that they can't pray—like, at all, other than a few sentences here and there.

Do you feel that way? That you're not good at prayer? That you can't pray or simply aren't good at it?

I love you, friend, but that's ridiculous. You know how to pray. That's a common accusation, and you've believed it.

Maybe you're reading this and are willing to press me a little. You would say, "No, I really don't know how to pray." Can you say, "God, I don't know how to pray, but I want to grow in prayer both in time spent and power in"? That's prayer! Can you say, "Help me, God, to know You and contend for my friends and family members against the enemy and his schemes"? That's prayer. "Protect me, God," or "Help me, God," or "Lead me into holiness"—that's prayer too.

My friend Jon Tyson says, "Pray what you got." If you believe you can't pray and agree with the lie, then you're not going to pray because you've convinced yourself you can't pray when all praying is is talking to God. This is the satanic lullaby, keeping you asleep. Prayer wreaks havoc in the spiritual world and accomplishes more than we can fathom. That's why the Dragon has to convince you that God doesn't delight in you. He has to stir up anger and hate in your heart for others.

If you wake up and start praying what you got, start praying simple prayers for your heart and hopes, and start spending time in the presence of Jesus, your enemy is done for—not just in you but even in those around you. The battlefield of your home, work, school, and the church needs your prayers. When you are praying for your soul and your family, friends, neighbors, and coworkers, you commit violence toward the Dragon's plans. It's fighting back, and it's what Overcomers do.

I encourage you to stop reading right now and pray what you got! What do you want Jesus to do in your life? Ask the Holy Spirit. Any specific fears or anxieties? Lay them at the feet of Jesus and ask the Holy Spirit for peace. Don't rush. My guess is you will immediately feel the enemy trying to pull you out of it. He's terrified that you'd enjoy the presence of Jesus and receive His peace and strength.

"YOU CAN'T UNDERSTAND THE BIBLE"

The other consistent accusation by Satan that many Christians believe is that they can't understand the Bible or that only the spiritual elite can know the Scriptures. Have you believed this? That you can't really understand the Bible?

Ephesians 6:17 calls the Bible the "sword of the Spirit." It's our weapon against the Dragon and his lies. I know you can read and understand the Bible. The Scriptures weren't only given to scholars; they were given to you.

Let me try to prove it to you. My guess is you can read and comprehend other things. Many of the men in the church I pastor have PhDs in the Dallas Cowboys. They know almost all the men who play for them, where those players played college ball, how fast they run, how high they jump, and even some info about their personal lives. They got that information by reading websites and watching videos online. If you have a hobby or a passion, you dig into it. You read books and articles on it, watch YouTube clips, and listen to audiobooks.

Why is the Bible different from that? It's different because those other things keep you asleep and docile. Prayerful study of God's Word makes you a warrior; it unleashes the mama bear and exposes the Dragon for what he is: defeated.

The accusations of "I don't know how to pray" and "I can't understand the Bible" keep hundreds of thousands of Christians asleep to the cosmic fight and trapped in nightmares of fear, powerlessness, and regret.

Are you asleep? Can you see the accusations of the Dragon in your own life? Do you believe you're welcome in the presence of God? That God wants to hear from you and speak to you? That the Holy Spirit will illuminate the Bible to you in ways that feed your soul and give you a weapon to spot the enemy's accusations and destroy them?

You might be hearing that satanic lullaby right now, singing over you that I'm wrong here, that your past or present struggles make you an outlier to these things. You think, *Sure, God might delight in people, but not me. I've gone too far. I've sinned in ways others haven't. He wants nothing to do with me.*

Friend, you're wrong. Moses killed a man with his bare hands and struggled with outbursts of rage most of his life. David was a murdering adulterer. Paul was a blasphemer and a violent man. God pulls from the fringes of darkness those who will be powerful lights.

Maybe that's not it; maybe you think your learning disorder keeps you from understanding. That's an accusation. It's not true.

I have to believe that, right now, the enemy is saying: "Shh. Just lie down. Shh. Go back to sleep. No, it's fine. Let your pastor know the Bible. Shh. He's got this." The compulsions when it's time to pray and read the Bible to turn on Netflix or check Instagram, or the tidal wave of thoughts around all the other things you need to get done, are part of this scheme. "Shh, go back to sleep," he says. But you should expect a spiritual fight.

So here's an idea: fight him. Open up your Bible and go, "I don't get it. I want to get it. Help me, Holy Spirit." Or swallow your pride and finally tell somebody, "I've been lazy, and I need somebody to help me." This is waking up. This is getting in the game.

Stop believing you don't know how to pray, that you don't know how to read your Bible, or that you're too dumb to share the gospel.

Stop it! It's a lie. It's his primary way of killing us. If you believe the accusations, you'll run from God rather than abide in His presence, and all the goodness of life is found in His presence. If you believe these accusations, you'll neglect the Scriptures, which are the sword of the Spirit.

You're going to be a spiritual powerhouse! I wish I were there to see it!

With the sword of the Spirit opened and the Holy Spirit illuminating the Scriptures, you will see how God defines you. Where you're from doesn't define you, your friends don't define you, your spouse and coworkers don't, your past doesn't, and your present doesn't. You are an Overcomer!

There's no condemnation for you. God is for you, not against you! No charge against you holds any weight! You have died with Christ, and your life is hidden with Christ in God.

You are more than a conqueror. Nothing can separate you from the love of God in Christ. You are a son or daughter of the King of the universe. You are royalty. It's not the elite who make war against the enemy. It's you.

Accusation gets its power from agreement. You have to be able to say, "That is not true about me."

We're so hostile and divided because the enemy has us hating ourselves and then accuses other people, and we believe it.

DECEIT

If accusation is the melody of the satanic lullaby, then deceit is the harmony. We read in Revelation 12 that the Dragon not only accuses but he also deceives. Verse 9 lets us know, "The great dragon was thrown down, that ancient serpent, who is called the devil and Satan, the deceiver of the whole world—he was thrown down to the earth, and his angels were thrown down with him." The deceiver of the whole world. Satan is good at deceiving, and it goes right along with his accusations.

When Satan deceives, it isn't just bad information. He wants you to feel a kind of way. It's not just knowing what's wrong; it's feeling something false. This isn't just "I believe this wrongly," although that is certainly a part. The Dragon is trying to get you to feel that God is holding out on you. He wants you to feel that God won't be enough. He wants you to question whether God is good and true to His word. He adds to, takes away from, twists, calls good *bad* and bad *good*, and has thousands of years of practice in deceiving, distorting, and taking what's rightfully ours.

The Dragon deceives in two primary ways. The first is false doctrine. It's believing about God things that aren't true. If you ever get the chance to go to the Museum of the Bible in Washington, DC, I highly recommend it. Among all the handwritten scrolls, ancient copies of texts, and other exhibits and experiences, you can see with your own eyes two "Bibles" that illustrate the way the Dragon deceives through false doctrine.

The first is the Jefferson Bible, created by Thomas Jefferson. Jefferson was a deist and didn't believe in the supernatural, but he deeply valued the philosophy of Jesus of Nazareth. He went line by line with a razor blade and glue through the four Gospels and other sections of the New Testament, removing all the miracles of Jesus, any claims of the deity of Jesus, and almost all mentions of the supernatural. Jefferson wanted a Jesus in his own image, not the Jesus of the Bible. The Jesus of the Bible is the incarnation of the second person of the Trinity. He's eternal and all-powerful. He demands a response.

To claim that Jesus was simply a teacher or philosopher requires you to ignore what He said about Himself. How can Jesus be a good teacher if what He taught has to be edited out? Jesus of Nazareth's being both fully God and fully man is how God has spoken to His creation once and for all.

You and I are not following the teaching of a moral philosopher. We're in a relationship with the God of the universe that was made possible by the life, death, and resurrection of Jesus Christ the Messiah, the King of the universe and Creator of all things.

The second "Bible" you could see at the Museum of the Bible is called the Slave Bible. The Slave Bible was produced by the Incorporated Society for the Conversion and Religious Instruction and Education of the Negro Slaves, and it removed all references to freedom and escape from slavery and oppression while emphasizing passages that taught submission and obedience. Once again, this unholy Bible's creators wanted to remake God in their image. They were denying the clear teaching of the imago Dei and justifying their compulsions and desires.

This is deceit, and it's still happening today. Tim Keller masterfully said:

> What happens if you eliminate anything from the Bible that offends your sensibility and crosses your will? If you pick and choose what you want to believe and reject the rest, how will you ever have a God who can contradict you? You won't! You'll have . . . a God, essentially, of your own making, and not a God with whom you can have a relationship and genuine interaction. Only if your God can say things that outrage you and make you struggle (as in a real friendship or marriage!) will you know that you have gotten hold of a real God and not a figment of your imagination.[3]

When we remake God in our image, we make Him weak and anxious like we are. As Overcomers, we love God and His moral law as He has revealed Himself in the Scriptures. He can be trusted because He's not just a philosopher but the Son of God. Our salvation and victory are certain not because He taught that they would be but because He was raised from the dead, assuring us that it is true.

The real Jesus is an inexhaustible well. The Dragon wants you to grow bored with Him. There are delights to be discovered and glories to be marveled in that will expand your worship and fuel your praise and gratitude. If the Dragon can keep you bored with Jesus or get you to doubt the goodness in His moral law, you become vulnerable to believing false things. The sheer volume of false teaching that's popping up online and on social media is staggering. Old heresies are being repackaged, and our culture's wicked values are defended by those calling themselves followers of Jesus.

The second way the Dragon uses deceit is to attack the church itself. If false doctrine deceives the individual, growing cold and bitter toward the bride of Christ is meant to steal unity and disrupt mission. The thing about the Dragon is he uses the same schemes with every generation; he just launches them from different platforms.

Regardless of the times in which you live, the church is both beautiful and a giant mess. The church is a place of deep healing and sometimes deep hurt. People have found lifelong, deep friendships built on grace and kindness, and they've been betrayed in ways that are hard to recover from.

As a local church pastor and the president of a large church planting organization, I constantly see and hear both stories. Praise God if you're part of a healthy local church and are taught well, encouraged in your gifts, and discipled into a greater awareness of Jesus' beauty and grace. That's what the church is meant to be: a living plausibility structure for the world to see the wisdom and beauty of God's design for human flourishing.

Where bad leadership is in place or God's grace isn't the binding value of a community, people get hurt. Every week, there's a new scandal involving the church or a leader in a church. Whole blogs, social media accounts, and podcasts have dedicated themselves to telling these stories. The Bible commands us to expose the works of darkness (Ephesians 5:11), so I'm grateful for where that has occurred. The sexual and spiritual abuse that's occurred in the church has defamed the name of Jesus and hurt people so deeply that they'll spend the rest of their earthly lives pursuing healing. This is a cause for outrage. I've felt deep sadness mixed with rage around some of the stories I have heard.

Those who still love Jesus after being abused and are seeking to serve others are a testimony of God's power to take what Satan meant for their destruction and weaponize it against him. The church needs reform in each generation, and those who love the church and hope to see her reformed in our day are allies and fellow Overcomers. Praise God for their tireless work and steadfast hope that a difference can be made.

As I mentioned above, I hear these stories all the time. I can understand the pull toward cynicism and rage. I've felt my own ability to give the benefit of the doubt fade.

In these moments, the beauty of the church pulls me back from the brink. As lead pastor of The Village Church, I've seen thousands of examples of the church being what she was meant to be. I've watched hundreds of children be fostered, the sick and dying loved and dignified, the broken welcomed and loved.

I've had a front-row seat to watch the redeeming power of Jesus work through imperfect people to bring about healing and restoration. No one is perfect, everyone is in process, and all of it is messy, but God's at work in the mess.

As a personal rule, if there isn't some balance between the good, right critique of the church and the joy-sustaining encouragement that comes from God's commitment to her, then I don't follow or give attention to them. I don't need help being cynical or jaded. Life is hard. We need each other to overcome consistently. We need a safe place that holds us accountable, helps us see clearly when things are foggy, provides direction for our lives when we feel lost in it all, and expects the greatness God has placed in us to shine.

Don't let the enemy deceive you into believing the church is your enemy. She's a mess at times, but she's beautiful too.

DEATH

I was thirty-four years old when I was told I had two to three years to live. At the time, that was the prognosis for someone with oligoden-droglioma WHO grade III. To say that it was a tough day would be underselling the pain, fear, and discombobulation of that conversation with my doctor. The last scheme of the enemy is the scheme of death itself.

In the first century, our brothers and sisters would hear the Dragon being described as red not as some sort of social death or some kind of marginalization from the predominant culture but as physical death. As in being killed, murdered. You might be thinking, *We went from accusation and deceit to murder?* I agree that escalated quickly, but it's the end-game of the Dragon to accuse you, deceive you, and keep you asleep until he can kill you.

The good news is you are an Overcomer, and that's not going to work either. Hebrews 2:14–15 says, "Since therefore the children share in flesh and blood, he himself [Jesus] likewise partook of the same things, that through death he might destroy the one who has the power of death, that is, the devil, and deliver all those who through fear of death were subject to lifelong slavery."

The Dragon tries to intimidate us with death, but Jesus has

disarmed him by making death gain. I know we don't like that. For goodness' sake! We're supposed to die when we're eighty-seven. Yet it's this freedom that makes us impervious to the enemy's attacks.

When you can spot the accusations, reject the deceit, and stand on the promises of God, you begin to walk in the courage you were designed to walk in. By the end of this book, I hope you can feel in the deepest places of your soul why the apostle Paul said, "To live is Christ, and to die is gain" (Philippians 1:21).

It's important to understand that mere Sunday morning attendance won't be enough for the fight we're in. There must be a robust ordering of our lives around the person, work, and beauty of Jesus Christ; a seriousness about spotting the accusations and deceit of the enemy; and embracing that death is gain. This kills fear and replaces it with Spirit-besotted courage.

I think you picked up this book because you want a life marked by courage and purpose. I pray as you look around at all the carnage the Dragon is causing, you feel provoked to fight back. I promise you he's terrified that you might wake up to this cosmic war and his schemes. As we head out to make war against the Dragon, it's important we understand how he fights, and the Spirit lays out his primary tactics for us to see.

I introduce you to the enemy's henchmen in Revelation. Scripture calls them beasts. Revelation 13 shows us how the cosmic battle plays out on earth. The first beast represents human kingdoms and reflects the beasts from Daniel 7. One of Satan's weapons against God's people is political power. It is not difficult for us to see how political issues harm the church and cause destruction. The second beast represents religious power. Its purpose is to get people to worship the first beast. This beast is also called the false prophet. He advocates compromise and putting our hope in things other than God. The Dragon and his beasts form an unholy trinity as a false representation of the Holy Trinity. As we are attacked by the enemy and his henchmen, we as Overcomers are not meant to be cruel or aggressive as we point out the sins of others, but we are to refuse to bow to the cultural pressures or live in isolation to avoid conflict. I then move on to the mark of the beast, one of the most talked about parts of Revelation. Since the book is apocalyptic, numbers mean something. As the numbers three and seven signify completion, the number 666 shows that the enemy is completely incomplete. Those siding with the Dragon are marked through their beliefs and actions. But we as Overcomers are marked by the Holy Spirit, which makes us look and act very differently from the world.

CHAPTER 8

THE HENCHMEN

Inigo Montoya loved watching his father, Domingo, work in his shop as a little boy. His father was a good man, a just man, and Inigo loved to watch his father apply his artistry to his trade.

One morning a client interested in his father's skill approached Domingo to ask about his services. Tyrone Rugen was a young, brash, and ambitious man, but he offered an incredible amount of money and the time necessary to create the perfect piece of art. Domingo reluctantly agreed and started to take Tyrone's measurements; it was then that he saw the sixth finger on Tyrone's right hand. The elder Montoya, a consummate professional, informed Rugen that the additional finger wouldn't affect the finished product.

For the next year, Domingo worked night and day in the shop, using the best materials possible to forge, fold, and create the perfect sword for the six-fingered man. Unfortunately, when Tyrone showed up to collect the sword, he offered Montoya only a tenth of what he had promised a year earlier. When Domingo refused, the future count in Prince Humperdinck's court stabbed Domingo in the heart with the sword he had created.

If this story sounds familiar to you, you've seen *The Princess Bride*. Young Inigo would spend the next twenty years looking for the "six-fingered man" to avenge his father's death. It ends with Inigo dueling with Count Rugen while citing his famous (at least among Gen Xers) introduction: "Hello, my name is Inigo Montoya. You killed my father. Prepare to die!"[1]

Count Tyrone Rugen isn't the primary antagonist in *The Princess Bride*. He's the henchman of the antagonist. He's an evil man who had a disturbing interest in the scientific study of pain and created a machine to suck the life out of a person. In other words, he is a sadist, deriving pleasure from inflicting pain on others. The evil he does, he does on behalf of another. He isn't calling the shots, but he is the active agent of evil on behalf of his lord.

In the previous chapter, we read about the Dragon and his schemes against God's people. If Revelation 12 shows us the cosmic battle between Satan and God's people (read *you*), then Revelation 13 shows us how that plays out on earth and the two primary henchmen of the Dragon.

THE FIRST BEAST— POLITICAL POWER

The book of Revelation is apocalyptic in its genre. That means images are used to provoke a deep response in the hearer. So as we look at these two henchmen, keep in mind the imagery is there to help you feel how evil and gross these henchmen are. The Bible calls them beasts.

The first beast is found in Revelation 13:1–10. It comes up out of the sea and looks like a mash-up of the beasts we see in Daniel 7. We don't have to guess what this beast represents because in Daniel 7:17–18, God told Daniel, "These four great beasts are four kings who shall arise out of the earth. But the saints of the Most High shall receive the kingdom and possess the kingdom forever, forever and ever." The beast in Daniel 7 represents the nations that would rule over the known world (Babylon, Persia, Mede, and ultimately Greece), so the beast is the embodiment of all that was expressed in the four beasts of Daniel 7—nations that would rule over the people of God.

The beast from the sea is the state—human kingdoms that have rejected the living God from the center of their lives. At the time John was writing, this beast was manifesting as Rome. We'll see this all the more clearly later on. Our brothers and sisters in AD 96 would've heard this and thought John was talking about Rome, and they weren't wrong. But it's not only Rome.

Before Rome, the beast manifested as Egypt, Assyria, and Babylon. John wanted us to see that a nation turns bestial when it sets out to be its own master. Power that is no longer exercised under God seeks to play God. I think history is pretty consistent here, and I believe we are watching it unfold in the Western world. Governments that turn their backs on the revealed moral law of God and His rule do not create cultures where humanity flourishes as they were designed. They don't become more divine; they become demonic. When a nation or culture exalts humanity as the measure of all things, those nations do not become more humane; they become more bestial.

Revelation highlights that one of the ways the Dragon wages war against the people of God is satanic-manipulated political power. The Dragon and his two beasts form an unholy trinity that mimics the actual triune God of the universe. The Dragon seeks to mimic God the Father, the first beast seeks to mimic God the Son, and the second beast seeks to mimic God the Holy Spirit. They mimic and mock and are a pathetic replacement for the actual triune God of the universe. We see this in Revelation 13:3, where there's a faux resurrection that causes everyone to start worshiping the beast—the government.

This isn't saying to be on the lookout for a world leader who resurrects; rather, it speaks of how hard the beast is to kill. The beast keeps coming back to claim more victims.

The beast was killed in World War II as the Allied forces stopped the Nazis' murder spree across Europe and resurrected almost immediately in the Communist regimes of the USSR, China, and Cambodia. In the twentieth century, the mass killings perpetrated by those governments measured between eighty-five and one hundred million people. As the USSR fell, other totalitarian regimes popped up worldwide. The Western world is growing more and more secular in its worldview and is becoming more bestial as a result. We'd be hard-pressed to argue that the Western world is growing in moral goodness that aligns with the laws of God.

The Dragon's plan through this beast is laid before us in verse 4: "And they worshiped the dragon, for he had given his authority to the beast, and they worshiped the beast, saying, 'Who is like the beast, and who can fight against it?'"

This is the endgame. The purpose of the beast isn't merely the exercise of political power. The objective is to capture the loyalties of men and women and divert them away from the worship of God. The way this beast fights isn't necessarily by throwing us into jail or killing us. It simply wants us to worship the state, to pull our loyalty away from Jesus and put it on something that cannot ultimately help us or save us. This is his game, and he's good at it.

I can only imagine the Dragon's pride toward this beast. He has easily ripped us to pieces over the past few years. The pressure to pick a political side is nearly impossible to avoid in the current cultural environment. The political right is correct to a point, and then they serve the Dragon. And the political left is correct to a point, and then they serve the Dragon.

The first beast is exceptional at drawing our allegiance away from Jesus and putting it on a political party or politician. It's going to sound right and feel right.

Didn't we all just have a front-row seat to this? In the past few years, how much anger, division, and despair have occurred in the United States? Everything became an issue to divide over, with each side putting its hope in a political party for the soul of the nation and the good of their families. I'm not saying policies don't matter. They do. Policies are about people, and people matter.

I'm talking about allegiance and unwavering hope. Be discerning where you place your hope. I'm not trying to turn you into a political cynic. If anyone shouldn't be cynical, it's us, but be careful. The state isn't the only way the Dragon seeks to destroy the children of God.

THE SECOND BEAST— RELIGIOUS POWER

We see right out of the gate in Revelation 13:11–18 that the purpose of the second beast is to get people to worship the first beast. The second beast seeks to get people to trust, follow, and worship political power that's moved out from under God. He performs great signs, creates an image of the first beast, and gives breath to it.

The second beast makes it very difficult for anyone who hasn't bowed down to the first beast. He can kill those who don't worship the image. He puts a mark on the people and makes it extremely difficult to buy, sell, or do business with the world unless they take on the mark.

In Revelation 16:13 and 19:20, this beast is called the "false prophet." If the beast from the sea is satanic-manipulated political power, the beast from the earth is satanic-manipulated religious power and institutions.

True prophets lead people to the worship of the living God. That's what they do. False prophets, and this one in particular, lead people to worship the state. This beast is advocating putting your hope in human means and institutions. That's all he does. He says, "Put your hope in this institution or program or political ideology. It'll save you. This will win the day. This is what's best for your children and grandchildren."

The second beast also encourages a compromise between Christians and culture. This beast argues that maybe we can make Christianity pretty for people. It whispers, "Wouldn't it be great if we were cool? If people saw us, they'd think, 'They're not that bad.'" This is the second beast negotiating a compromise.

About six years into my pastorate at The Village, I received an email from a man I'd never met named Shawn. The email was filled with curses and accusations. He called me a bigot, a homophobe, and about fifteen other things I can't share here. A student at Dallas Theological Seminary had given him an iPod (remember those?) filled with my sermons, and upon listening to them, he was furious that I'd called homosexuality a sin. He even went as far as accusing me of causing teenagers to kill themselves.

I wasn't used to taking this kind of email beating from strangers back then and felt compelled to set up a lunch with him. He agreed as long as he could bring a friend. We met for lunch in Oak Lawn in Dallas, and for nearly three hours I heard stories of cruelty and rejection that frustrated my soul, saddened my heart, and enraged me for how their interactions with the people of God had played out. It was terrible, sinful, and gross.

I apologized on behalf of my brothers and sisters who had sinned against Shawn and his friend and circled back around with the message of the gospel. This began a friendship between Shawn and me that was one of the stranger experiences of my life. I met his partner of more than twenty years, David, and was consistently invited into his world. He had a beautiful spirit and quick wit and loved to debate. I genuinely enjoyed his company.

About a year into our friendship, Shawn invited me to dinner so a group of his gay friends could ask me questions. He confessed that it could go badly, but he thought it might help heal some of their anger and bitterness. I don't know if I've ever been so nervous going into something. We ate dinner, got to know one another, and laughed a lot. It was cordial and relaxed. Then the questions started. They started friendly enough. A young man asked if he'd be welcome at The Village, and I assured him he would be. I even told him he could sit with my family if he liked.

The next question was about our denominational affiliation—a softball question—and then all hell broke loose. They asked whether I believed homosexuality was a sin. I explained that everyone is sexually bent and broken. All of us have sexual compulsions that have to be submitted to the God of the Bible. The young man pressed me with the same question again, and I stated clearly that I believed what the church has believed since the beginning and what the Scriptures clearly state: homosexuality is a sin. I've never been as verbally assaulted as I was in the next thirty to forty-five minutes.

Looking back, it was naive to begin with. I felt ambushed and foolish. I didn't hate those men. On the contrary, I had a great deal of compassion for them and loved the time we shared telling stories about our hopes and frustrations.

The next day, Shawn texted me a question about taking the Lord's Supper at The Village. I told him he wouldn't be able to take part in it because he wasn't a Christian. He went berserk, accusing me of withholding Communion because he was gay. I asked him if he believed Jesus was the Son of God who died for his sins and if he had submitted to Him as the Lord of his life. He told me he believed that Jesus thought He was the Son of God, dropped a few explicit words, and hung up on me.

I didn't hear from him for several months until he showed up at one of our Saturday night services. It was clear he was testing The Village Church's willingness to be welcoming, and I was proud of the men and women of The Village that night. Despite Shawn acting ridiculously, they interacted with him, made space for him, and put up with his mean jabs.

After the service, he let me know he'd been diagnosed with cancer and would be starting treatment in Dallas.

Shawn's body was decimated by the chemo, the radiation, and the cancer itself for the next year and a half. He died at home with his partner and his mom. I attended his funeral and wept.

I'm telling this story because I loved Shawn, enjoyed my time with him, and learned a lot from him. I hated how the church had treated him and his mother when he was growing up. The pull in my heart to back off what I knew to be true was powerful. Knowing what the church has believed and taught for thousands of years didn't stop clouds of doubt from forming in my mind. I'd think, *Shawn is a good man. He might just be a better man than some of the church members I pastor.* The temptation to buy into shoddy scholarship and textual gymnastics so I didn't have to say homosexuality is a sin pulled hard on my heart.

I'm telling you this story because I believe you will feel what I'm describing as the second beast. Did you feel nervous as you read the story? Find yourself wishing I hadn't put it in the book? Are you worried about a friend? The second beast does this—this is the pull of compromise.

Compromise with the world is never loving and is actually quite cruel. Where we have relationships with others, we must always remain faithful to Jesus and the Scriptures that lead us into His good designs for us. If you remember back to the letters to the churches in Revelation 2–3, this was the biggest temptation, the thing that was going to cause lampstands to be removed: compromising with the first century's pagan sexual ethics (2:14, 20).

Being an Overcomer isn't about being brash, being cruel, or aggressively pointing out the sins of others. It's refusing to bow to the cultural pressures of our day either by rejecting the historical teachings of the church and Scripture or by closing the doors of your home and living in fear of the rejection of the world.

MARKED BY THE BEAST?

Few things have captured the world's imaginations quite like the "mark of the beast" in Revelation. In movies, heavy metal album covers, and scary stories, the number 666 is used to create a sense of darkness and evil. It's the second beast that gives the mark.

Revelation 13:16–18 says:

Also it [the beast] causes all, both small and great, both rich and poor, both free and slave, to be marked on the right hand or the forehead, so that no one can buy or sell unless he has the mark, that is, the name of the beast or the number of its name. This calls for wisdom: let the one who has understanding calculate the number of the beast, for it is the number of a man, and his number is 666.

The big question that's led to quite a bit of creativity in the Christian community is, What is the mark of the beast? The latest guesses have included the COVID-19 vaccine and something with our phones. There's been a long line of guesses over the past two thousand years, and they've all missed. I recently had lunch with a friend who told me he read an article about a chip designed to be placed in your hand by which you can buy and sell. Could that be the mark? Maybe, but I don't think so. Let me explain why.

Remember, Revelation is apocalyptic, so numbers mean something. As we saw in the letters to the seven churches, the number seven is the number for completeness. It's related to God, not man. God is seven; man is six. Man is incomplete next to God's completeness. The Dragon and the two beasts mimic the triune God of the universe, the one who sits on the throne at the center of reality.

Three is also a number meaning complete. Three sixes mean completely incomplete. The number 666 signifies that our enemy is completely incomplete.

The hand and the forehead are also significant in how God molds and forms His people. If you remember the Shema in Deuteronomy 6, the people of God were meant to have the law of God written on their hands and doorposts and gates and to wear it on their foreheads (vv. 8–9). When they rose and when they woke, they were looking at the Law.

The mark's location is about ideology and action. When we're talking about the mark of the beast, we're talking about the internal character made manifest in behavior. G. K. Beale rightly pointed out, "The 'forehead' represents ideological commitment and the 'hand' the practical outworking of that commitment."[2]

The mark of the beast is here now. Those who reject the true Creator God and align themselves with the mimicking Dragon and beasts bear the mark through their ideological beliefs and actions.

It's important to remember we've been marked too. The first three verses of Revelation 7 say:

> After this I saw four angels standing at the four corners of the earth, holding back the four winds of the earth, that no wind might blow on earth or sea or against any tree. Then I saw another angel ascending from the rising of the sun, with the seal of the living God, and he called with a loud voice to the four angels who had been given power to harm earth and sea, saying, "Do not harm the earth or the sea or the trees, until we have sealed the servants of our God on their foreheads."

We are marked too. We've been sealed with the Holy Spirit. We belong to God. It's not earthly ideologies that drive us—it's heavenly love. That's how we're able to stand against the world for the sake of the world.

FIGHTING BEASTS

I recently started training in Brazilian jiujitsu with my son, Reid. On our first night at the gym, we learned a few moves, practiced them without resistance, and spent the last twenty minutes of class "rolling." *Roll* is the word for sparring in jiujitsu. It's where you practice the various moves learned and how to stay calm in a fight. Two things are true in Brazilian jiujitsu: (1) regardless of the size of your opponent, you have to take them seriously, and (2) with the proper patience, training, and moves, you can beat a much larger, stronger opponent.

This is also true about overcoming the two henchmen of the Dragon. When I look at the volume of deceit, depression, fear, manipulation, death, and chaos that this mimicking unholy trinity perpetuates on my friends, family, coworkers, and the world around me, my impulse is anger and a desire to fight back. I hate the two henchmen. I want to hit back.

But I know I need to take them seriously. They're extraordinarily powerful and have had thousands of years honing their craft. Yet with the proper patience, training, and moves, we can become a real problem for these evil powers behind the world's sorrows.

It's important to remember that the two henchmen are our enemies. The apostle Paul told us in Ephesians 6:12, "We do not wrestle against flesh and blood, but against the rulers, against the authorities, against the cosmic powers over this present darkness, against the spiritual forces of evil in the heavenly places."

Our enemies aren't the men and women stuck in their web. God has invited us to help participate in their rescue.

Now that we know who our enemies are, how do we fight? There are four primary moves we use as Overcomers to fight back.

HOLINESS

Overcomers seriously pursue holiness. Holiness is hating sin and loving righteousness. When I talk about hate, I'm talking about violence against sin—our sin. We don't fight back by being experts in other people's sins but ours. The book of Hebrews tells us that sin easily entangles and weighs down (12:1). How can you fight if you're entangled and weighed down? You can't.

Is there anything popping up in your mind right now? Are there small things that don't seem to be that big of a deal to you, but you know they don't please God? I get that these can feel like no big deal, but they are cracks in your armor against the enemy and leave you exposed. We fight not only by not doing evil but by filling our lives with the fuel of worship and gladness.

I love this quote from Tim Chester:

> The difference between the person who grows in holiness and the one who doesn't is not a matter of personality, upbringing, or gifting. The difference is what each has planted into the soil of his heart and soul, so holiness isn't a mysterious spiritual state that only an elite few can reach. It's more than an emotion or a resolution or an event. Holiness is a harvest.[3]

What are you sowing into your life? What seeds are you dropping into your soul every day that in time might produce a harvest of holiness? I have some thoughts on cultivating a life of holiness and how you sow these seeds—the first I already mentioned.

I won't give sin a foothold in my life, no matter how embarrassing.

On July 3, 1991, several friends and I rushed to the movie theater to see *Terminator 2*. The movie was about two cyborgs from the future sent back in time. One was sent to kill John Connor; the other was sent to save him.

Terminator 2 is a movie in a long line of stories about how artificial intelligence leads to humanity's dark, apocalyptic future. Whether it was *2001: A Space Odyssey*, *Ex Machina*, or the Matrix films, the story is the same: computers come to life and start to hunt and kill us.

The irony is, artificial intelligence is hunting and killing us, but in ways that we aren't paying attention to. A robot kicking in my door with a futuristic weapon is one thing, but the gentle pull to look at my phone for the six thousandth time or binge yet another series is something altogether different.

The robot with the weapon would create dread and have my defenses up. The algorithm that's learned what I want to see and how long I can scroll or watch until I need my dopamine triggered and keeps me marinating in mediocrity is just my life.

Did you know it would take you ninety-nine hours to binge-watch *The Office* and another ninety-nine hours to watch the entire Marvel franchise? If you're more of a *Star Wars* person, that's 131 hours.

Pay Attention

A recent study revealed we touch our phones over 2,600 times a day.[4] That's a lot of input. How much of our scrolling, watching, listening, and bingeing is forming us into the fearless, faith-filled Overcomers we're meant to be?

Don't get me wrong: I love living in this technological age. I like my phone and the ease of streaming a movie or show. These are graces of God, but if we're not careful, they also can become a demonic pacifier putting us back to sleep.

What stirs your affections for Jesus and His kingdom? If you can answer that question, begin to fill your life with more of it. What robs you of your affections for Jesus and His kingdom? These can be morally neutral or even good but still pull your attention and affection away from Jesus. If you can answer that question and begin to limit those things, you're beginning to cultivate holiness in your life.

What we give our minds and thoughts to with great repetition grows us into wickedness or holiness.

Seek Accountability

Another way to plant seeds of holiness in your soul is to surround yourself with friends who are equally or more serious about Jesus and His kingdom. I need encouragement and people to engage with my blind spots because I can't see them.

One of the best things I did as a young pastor was invite a group of men in proximity to watch over my life. I asked them to pay attention and see whether they saw inconsistencies in me, especially between my preaching and my life. I *invited* the accountability. I asked them to help guard me and my heart. I'm human, prone to wander, pulled by pride and foolishness. I asked these men to hem me in and fight with me and for me.

You need a little platoon. You need to invite people in. Encourage godly friends to help you. You need people to watch your life. You have blind spots. You have to invite them in for this purpose: to watch and encourage and engage you when you start to drift. You need to invite them in because, generally speaking, people are scared of conflict or love conflict, and both are bad. You're not asking somebody to be nit-picky about your life. You're asking for spiritual encouragement and protection.

Overcomers act violently toward our sins and sinful compulsions by dragging them into the light. There's no room for sin, no matter how big or small. All sin is tied back to the Dragon and two beasts, and we remember that we're in a cosmic war.

Holiness is fostered by paying attention to what our inputs are. As Overcomers, we understand that whatever we give our minds and hearts to with repetition spiritually shapes us. As Overcomers, we enjoy God's good graces but guard our inputs and then establish new ones that cultivate zeal for Jesus and delight in His goodness and grace. We pay attention to what stirs our affections for Jesus and what robs us of that affection.

Holiness is a communal project. Overcomers form little platoons of other Christians, inviting them both to encourage them and engage them in their blind spots when necessary. Overcomers fight the hench-man of the Dragon by seriously pursuing holiness, but this isn't our only weapon.

CONFESSION AND REPENTANCE

Do you have secret sin that you've hidden now or in your past? Maybe you've promised yourself you won't let anybody know; you're taking it to the grave. You're convinced that your whole world would burn to the ground if you were to confess whatever it is.

Here's the good news: your life is in God's hands; it isn't your world. Do you want to fight? Confess. Drag whatever it is into the light. Did you have an affair a decade ago, steal money at work, become addicted to drugs or pornography, get secretly drunk, swipe left and hook up, betray a good friend, or consistently dwell on doubt?

Whatever it is, confess it out loud to God and then find a group of other Overcomers and confess it to them. That's your first shot across the jaw of the enemy. Now you're a problem to the devil. He can't use shame to keep you quiet and afraid anymore.

I know that confession can cause a lot of hurt and pain. I'm not naive. I've been doing ministry for close to thirty years, and I've seen that to be 99 percent known is to be unknown.

Secret sin and shame bind and lock a person out of the fight. Psalm 32:3 says, "When I kept silent [about my sins], my bones wasted away through my groaning all day long." Do you know what it would feel like just to get it off you?

Do you know how much of a problem you'll be to the enemy with just a confession of your sin? That in and of itself is a declaration of war. When you confess and repent, you state that the enemy no longer gets to occupy your heart, mind, home, and relationships and no longer gets to accuse, shame, or shackle you. It's a declaration that you plan to take the fight to him rather than sit back and take jabs from him. No more. That day is over.

Darkness loses power in the light. It doesn't mean the journey is easy. When we sin, there can be significant collateral damage. But it does mean we can get untangled and out from under the soul-crushing weight of sin. There are no small sins, just sins waiting to destroy everything you're serious about loving.

That's why I'm trying to wake you up to the fight. It's trying to destroy you.

Pursuing holiness and the ongoing ethics of confession and repentance are our primary weapons against the henchmen that seek to kill and destroy us. We confess our sins. The life of a Christian is one of ongoing confession and repentance. This is our primary weapon.

PRAYER AND WORSHIP

A story from 1 Samuel 16 has captivated my attention since I first read it decades ago. The Spirit of the Lord had departed from King Saul, and a "harmful spirit" was tormenting him (v. 14). The demonic spirit would send Saul into deep emotional and physical pain, and it would rest on him until David played the lyre.

When David played to the Lord, the Bible says, "Saul was refreshed and was well, and the harmful spirit departed from him" (v. 23). When David worshiped God with song, this demon departed, and Saul was refreshed.

When we gather to pray on Sunday mornings at The Village, I always ask if the Holy Spirit will do this same thing: weaken the demonic holds on people and refresh their souls as we sing and make much of Jesus. Overcomers fight with prayer and worship. One of the more underrated weapons God has given you against the enemy is prayer and worship, and it's telling that the church as a whole seems to struggle with these two things.

When the Bible talks about worship, it's not simply talking about singing, although that's a powerful part of it. Worship is attention. Whenever we fix our attention or order our lives so that our attention is on Him, that's worship.

When it comes to prayer, I've found this quote from C. Peter Wagner helpful:

> God's purpose may be thwarted, or it may be accomplished depending, to one degree or another, on the obedience of his people and their willingness to use the weapons of spiritual warfare that He has provided. God is powerful enough to win any battle, but He has designed things so that the release of His power at a given moment of time often is contingent upon the decisions and the actions of his people. A principal weapon of spiritual warfare is prayer. Not just routine or mediocre prayer, but prayer powerful enough to move God's hand in order to determine the destiny of a whole nation.[5]

Don't go back now and begin to think you lack the eloquence and your prayers probably fall into the routine or mediocre category Wagner mentioned. You can pray powerful prayers. Powerful enough to move God's hand.

Start by simply praying, *God, I don't know how to pray like this. I'd love to pray in such a way that it moves Your hand and I join You in what You are accomplishing in my day.* Look at you! You're a prayer-warring freak! It'll grow from that heart cry in both time and effectiveness.

In Matthew 6, Jesus warned against praying so that others would see you and marvel at how good you are at praying. He also warned against praying with "empty phrases as the Gentiles do, for they think that they will be heard for their many words" (v. 7). You don't have to be the wisest or most eloquent. You don't have to have the most words—just an honest heart before God. A simple, "Help, please . . . I want to receive Your love and be a conduit through which it flows to other people."

That's a big-time prayer in God's economy. We fight by seriously pursuing holiness with ongoing confession and repentance and with prayer and worship.

HOMES AND TABLES

In Rosaria Champagne Butterfield's excellent book *The Gospel Comes with a House Key*, she said:

> Instead of feeling sidelined by the sucker punches of post-Christianity, Christians are called to practice radically ordinary hospitality to renew their resolve in Christ. Too many of us are sidelined by fears. We fear that people will hurt us. We fear that people will negatively influence our children. We fear that we do not even understand the language of this new world order, least of all its people. We long for days gone by. Our sentimentality makes us stupid. We need to snap ourselves out of this self-pitying reverie. The best days are ahead. Jesus advances from the front of the line.[6]

Overcomers practice radically ordinary hospitality as a weapon against evil and despair in this present darkness. Compromise happens when we cater to the predominant culture's values that stand opposed to the reign and rule of Jesus.

Compromise also happens when we choose our own comfort and control over the mission of God to love and serve those who are far from God. When we talk about hospitality, we aren't talking about some peonies on the table with votive candles or some bread baking when they come in. There's nothing wrong with those things, and beauty is a powerful apologetic, but hospitality is more than having friends over for dinner. That's more entertainment. Entertainment frequently has more to do with the host than the guest.

Hospitality looks like this:

You have heard that it was said, "Love your neighbor and hate your enemy." But I tell you, love your enemies and pray for those who persecute you, that you may be children of your Father in heaven. He causes his sun to rise on the evil and the good, and sends rain on the righteous and the unrighteous. If you love those who love you, what reward will you get? Are not even the tax collectors doing that? And if you greet only your own people, what are you doing more than others? Do not even pagans do that? (Matthew 5:43–47 NIV)

The idea of hospitality, specifically hospitality as the Bible defines it, is welcoming the stranger. You and I have been immersed in stranger danger our whole lives. We're terrified of others or indifferent, and biblical hospitality is a welcoming of the stranger or maybe even the enemy. There's no space for that, because I think these two beasts have done such a number on us in our day that it just sounds unreasonable.

I love this quote by Stephen Rhodes:

Hospitality, when you get right down to it, is unnatural. It is difficult to place others first, because our inclination is to take care of ourselves first. Hospitality takes courage. It takes a willingness to risk. But as our Lord reminds us, if we only love those who we are sure will love us and welcome those who will welcome us, then we have done little to share the love of God, for as Jesus says, even the heathen do that. Hospitality is being received openly, warmly, freely, without any need to prove ourselves. Hospitality makes us feel worthy, because our host assumes we are worthy. This is the kind of hospitality that we have experienced from God, and all that God asks is that we go and do likewise, particularly to "the alien among us."[7]

How are you currently doing against these henchmen? What other tactics are you employing to play not just defense but offense? Are you taking the fight to them or hoping just to stay out of their way? They should be more nervous about you, remember?

THE REAL THING

How do we make war against the beasts?

Not with their weapons. Not with violence. Not with shaming. Not with mocking. Not with belittling. That isn't how we make war. To do so would be to join the beasts in what they're doing and become like them.

What is our call? Faithful endurance. What does it look like? It looks like confession of sin and violently putting sin to death in our lives. To fight is to confess, to repent, to fill our lives with worship and prayer, and it looks like hospitality. It looks like dining room tables with people who are different from us sitting around them so that we might show them the love of God that we've received as His people. These things must be woven into the makeup of our lives.

I begin by sharing about a time when I was struck by the deep belief that some men and women have that Jesus is on His throne and worthy of their lives. We are part of a great family of faith, as shown in Revelation 14. It tells of the 144,000 who are faithful to the Father. We are counted among them. As discouraging as life may be, we must remember that we are not alone as we walk the narrow path. I ask that you remember our origin story and where we'd be if the Spirit hadn't touched our lives. We are in fact part of an origin story that goes back to Acts 1:15. Scripture encourages us that we're not alone in walking this journey and fighting this war against the enemy. We have help. As we join God's plan of salvation in sharing the gospel with the lost, we have the Holy Spirit and angelic armies. The angels in Revelation proclaim the gospel, the fall of Babylon, and God's wrath. I remind you that as we think about judgment and wrath, we do not want an indifferent God who allows sin and Satan to go unaddressed. We can be thankful that God in His righteous judgment reigns. And we must be prayerful and be ready to give others an answer for the hope we have in a hurting and broken world.

CHAPTER 9

A MASSIVE AND MIGHTY ARMY

One of the more exciting things I've had the privilege of doing has been training house church pastors in a couple of countries where following Jesus could get you put into prison or killed.

Several years ago, I left my hotel room around midnight to get in a van and drive a few hours to a farmhouse in the middle of nowhere. I was shown to a small bedroom with a cot and several blankets and crawled into it around 2:30 in the morning and fell asleep fast, but not for long.

At 3:42 a.m., I woke to the sound of singing in the room next to mine. I didn't recognize the words or the tune, but I knew the angst of the sound. Soul-level singing to Jesus was going on in the other room, and it was getting louder and louder. I laid there and listened for the next hour, hoping I could fall back asleep to it. I was scheduled to teach for ten to twelve hours that day and wanted to get as much rest as possible.

Over that next hour, the volume of their singing increased, and I could tell the numbers were swelling. I asked the Holy Spirit to be my strength and got up and dressed for the day. When I walked out of my room and into the large gathering space where we would meet for the next couple of days, I could tangibly feel the presence of God there. It's one of just a handful of moments in my life when I was aware I was in a holy place.

None of the thirty to forty men and women had a dry eye. Hands were raised, and faces bowed into the dirt floor; some people were laughing while others were crying. Over the next couple of days, I'd learn that many of them hadn't seen each other in years, others had just been released from jail, and none had sung loudly in a group that size in a long, long time.

I was struck by how much I take for granted at the church I pastor. How singing loudly and without fear is just what we do. I sat there and watched them for the next several hours. When a new pastor would show up, they'd immediately move to embrace them and pray over them, and they would join in.

On more than one occasion, the pastor simply collapsed into the group of welcoming prayers and wept uncontrollably. It was one of the more beautiful things I've ever seen. I would rather have stayed in that state for the rest of our time together. The thought of my teaching adding value to what the Holy Spirit was up to in that room seemed silly. The people who made this happen knew the need and brought me there to teach and encourage.

Around 6 a.m., we had breakfast and then settled in for the morning block of teaching. I'm not sure I've taught to a more eager and attentive group. As we broke for lunch, different pastors began to share testimonies of what they saw in their congregations. Men and women were being saved; sick people were being healed. There were stories of believers being thrown in jail and other stories of believers being tortured.

I learned not to romanticize the difficulty of those following Jesus in places like this. Some men and women broke down and wept as they shared the difficulties they'd endured. One pastor hadn't seen his family in over a year. As hardships were shared, the room moved toward the pastor, surrounded them, and began interceding. Cries for strength and courage and the Holy Spirit's power over them were prayed, a few songs were sung, and someone else would share.

I taught the rest of the day, and that night we sat around a fire and shared hopes, dreams, frustrations, and things we were grateful for. At some point, I tried to say a word in their language, and the whole group began to laugh hysterically. Someone else would give me a word to say, and I'd try to pronounce it, and the group would laugh all the more. After a while, I gave them an English word, and then I'd laugh. No one there could say the word *welcome*, and I laughed until my cheeks hurt hearing them try.

As we played that game, it struck me that these were simply men and women like you and me. They had families, friends, jobs, and hobbies, and they loved to laugh and play. They were captivated by Jesus and His beauty and were still very much human. They were afraid and sad and anxious at times, but on fire for the kingdom of God. They *believed* in their bones that Jesus was on the throne and was worthy of their lives.

Although this experience was an outlier in my travels, by the grace of God, I've been able to worship with men and women in Asia, the Middle East, Rwanda, Kenya, South Africa, Brazil, Spain, South Sudan, and more. All over the world, there are men and women following zealously after Jesus, praising Jesus, worshiping Jesus, trusting Him through the hard stuff, rejoicing in His provision and grace, and asking Him to save family and friends. I'm not sure if you've thought much about this, but it's pretty amazing that there are 2.38 billion Christians worldwide.[1] I know we're looking around our reality here in the West and thinking all is broken, but you belong to a global and eternal family.

OUR FAMILY OF FAITH

After showing us our enemy and his schemes in the mimicking trinity of the Dragon and two beasts, John encouraged us again by showing us our family of faith. Revelation 14:1–5 says:

> Then I looked, and behold, on Mount Zion stood the Lamb, and with him 144,000 who had his name and his Father's name written on their foreheads. And I heard a voice from heaven like the roar of many waters and like the sound of loud thunder. The voice I heard was like the sound of harpists playing on their harps, and they were singing a new song before the throne and before the four living creatures and before the elders. No one could learn that song except the 144,000 who had been redeemed from the earth. It is these who have not defiled themselves with women, for they are virgins. It is these who follow the Lamb wherever he goes. These have been redeemed from mankind as firstfruits for God and the Lamb, and in their mouth no lie was found, for they are blameless.

This is the same thing we saw in Revelation 7:4: our great family of faith across time and space. After all this talk about the Dragon and beasts, we need this reminder.

The number 144,000 represents completeness. All the saints across history joined before the throne singing a "new song" that sounds like the "roar of many waters and like the sound of loud thunder" and "like the sound of harpists playing on their harps." According to the Vienna Symphonic Library, the sound of a harp is "gentle, rushing, brilliant, flowing, crystal clear, reverberating, splashing and cascading."[2] I'm not quite sure what that will sound like, but the Spirit wants us to know it is *loud* and *big*.

We also see in this passage that these are men and women who remained loyal as a bride to Jesus. The symbolism of virginity here is used in multiple places to reference those who refuse to commit acts of spiritual adultery with the Dragon and the beasts (2 Kings 19:21; Isaiah 37:22; 2 Corinthians 11:2). You and I are counted among this throng of souls. We're marked by Jesus as Overcomers, hearts that have given their attention and worship to Him and by His grace have refused to commit spiritual adultery. Don't be discouraged by this present moment. You belong to a global and eternal family made up of every tribe, tongue, and nation on earth. A family so big that "no one could number" us (Revelation 7:9).

I know the road is narrow that leads to salvation, but billions and billions of people have walked that narrow path.

And you're one of them.

THE ORIGIN STORY

I still remember going to see *The Empire Strikes Back* in the theater as a kid. Regardless of the storyline, I found myself cheering for Darth Vader. Luke was too whiny for me and Han too cocky, so that left Vader. His music, his costume, and the ease at which he handled his enemies drew me to him. He was ruthless, powerful, and did I mention his music and costume? It was too much for my seven-year-old self, and Vader became my guy.

Throughout the original three films, we got bits and pieces of his backstory, but it took twenty-five years and three terrible prequels before we understood how Anakin Skywalker rejected the Force, swore allegiance to Palpatine, and laid waste to the Jedi temple before a duel with Obi-Wan left him dismembered, burned alive, and filled with hate and rage.

In our movies, books, and shows, there's almost always a moment where we get filled in on the main character's backstory. How did they get to this moment in the story that is entertaining us? What made them so optimistic, pessimistic, good at fighting, oriented around justice, out for revenge, or whatever it may be?

You have a backstory. It's important that you remember it. Specifically, I want you to take a few minutes to remember your salvation. When did you surrender your life to Jesus as your Lord and Savior? What was going on before? How did you become aware that you needed a Savior? Was your life falling apart, or did the Spirit reveal Jesus' saving work to you as a child? Were you stuck in dead, religious self-righteousness or were you pretty deep into the party scene?

Maybe it's something completely different, but I want you to think about your origin story for a moment. Where would you be in this moment if the Spirit hadn't opened your eyes to the beauty and grace of Jesus?

Every one of the billions and billions of men and women who make up our family of faith has a backstory similar to yours in that they were outside the kingdom of God and were transferred by the mercy of God into the life, death, and resurrection of Jesus. How did the gospel go from 120 Jewish believers at Jesus' ascension (Acts 1:15) to the 2.3 billion we see globally in our day spread across all seven continents? It certainly hasn't happened by the schemes of humankind.

Faithful Overcomers in each generation joined with the Spirit of God and angels to share the good news with those in proximity to them. Some traveled oceans and engaged unreached peoples, but most heard of salvation from a friend or family member. Your origin story goes all the way back to that moment in Acts 1:15.

In a thousand turns in history, God faithfully called you to Himself through the prayerful courage of the Overcomers who preceded you.

It's our turn now. What will we do with our days?

SUPERNATURAL HELP

In Revelation 14:6–9, we see three angels that fly over the earth and make various proclamations. In each case, they herald the gospel to earth's inhabitants. They are doing the work of evangelism.

Despite hearing many stories of conversion where the man or woman had a dream, visitation, or other supernatural experience, I don't believe that what we see here is angels doing the work as much as we're seeing that the work of evangelism and conversion aren't mere natural acts but have supernatural power. When we're bold enough to open our lives and mouths and share the good news of the gospel with friends, family members, and neighbors, we have angelic, supernatural help. This is important because many of us shy away from sharing because we feel we don't know enough and might get asked a question we can't answer or that we aren't quick enough on our feet to have those spiritual-level conversations.

The good news is, we aren't alone in it. The Spirit inside you will remind you of things you've learned or heard, like an angel flying directly overhead proclaiming the gospel. Something supernatural is in the air. Look at 14:6–7:

> Then I saw another angel flying directly overhead, with an eternal gospel to proclaim to those who dwell on earth, to every nation and tribe and language and people. And he said with a loud voice, "Fear God and give him glory, because the hour of his judgment has come, and worship him who made heaven and earth, the sea and the springs of water."

Notice who the angel is proclaiming the gospel to: "those who dwell on earth." Remember that phrase from earlier? The proclamation is going out to those who have rejected or never heard of Jesus as Lord and Savior. There's still time for them.

Notice the breadth of the invitation: "every nation and tribe and language and people." The proclamation and invitation are global. What's your favorite place you've ever visited? The gospel is being proclaimed there. Where have you always wanted to go? What place is on your bucket list? The gospel is being proclaimed there. Where do you want to avoid at all costs? The gospel is being proclaimed there. Is there a language you wish you were fluent in? The gospel is being proclaimed in that language. Is there a culture you are fascinated with? The gospel is being proclaimed there.

Jesus taught in Matthew 24 that "this gospel of the kingdom will be proclaimed throughout the whole world as a testimony to all nations, and then the end will come" (v. 14). The work of heralding the gospel is where Overcomers join in with God's plan to seek and save the lost from all over the world.

You're holding this book in your hand because someone before you joined in with this angel and told you with some variation of language to "fear God and give him glory." You were told God is the Creator of all things and you should repent and worship Him. The Spirit opened your eyes to believe, and you joined the 144,000 marked by Jesus and sealed with the Spirit. I've been saying it on repeat, but it's our moment to join in with God's drawing men and women unto Himself.

Don't buy the lie that we can be neutral about this.

Switzerland and Ireland are a couple of European countries that have decided not to join the North Atlantic Treaty Organization (NATO) and instead stay neutral in the world's conflicts. These two nations don't consider themselves great powers on the world stage and choose to sit out the many wars other nations get pulled into.

The pull of our day is not to participate in God's mission to seek and save the lost but instead to be neutral. There's a deformed kind of Christianity in our day that doesn't dislike God but is embarrassed by some of what He says and tries to just stay out of it all. These Christians desire to be good, moral, churchgoing people who let others live the way they want to live as long as it isn't hurting anybody else.

This is a type of spiritual neutrality that doesn't exist. To be indifferent to the lostness of humankind and the good news that there's a way to be reconciled with one's Creator is the way of the Dragon.

There are only two sides, and everyone is on one.

Unlike Switzerland, you *are* a major player in this great conflict. Remember that you've been uniquely wired and placed so people might seek him and find him.

AIR WAR AND GROUND WAR

At The Village, we take time each October to do a large prayer walking initiative. We encourage each person or family to find a couple of nights a week and repetitive walk their neighborhoods to pray simple blessings over their neighbors' homes. They ask Jesus to bring peace over the house, depth and beauty to the marriage represented, safety for the kids who live there, salvation if the residents aren't believers, and gladness to the home.

This might sound small, but this is cosmic warfare. The prayers of the saints are loosening strongholds. I assure you that the principalities and powers don't think it's a small deal. On the contrary, I imagine they begin to shudder in panic. The Overcomers are joining in God's offensive against darkness and destruction. Things are being moved in the heavenlies.

The days in Texas are long in October, and the temperatures have finally come down from their brutal summer highs. It's not uncommon to see neighbors out front or out for a walk themselves. Our members are encouraged to let their neighbors know what they're doing and ask for any specifics around how they can pray. This simple act has led to those far from God asking their neighbors to pray for their marriage struggles, fears with children, the healing of a sick family member, or the person's current struggle with life in general.

We pray in the moment for them and then, if possible, exchange contact information. From there we pray fervently and check in occasionally. This usually leads over time to dinner and deeper relationships and conversations. If praying over houses in our neighborhoods is the air war, these conversations and dinners become the ground war for the souls of humankind.

By the grace of God we've watched in awe as God has saved those far from Him with this simple act of defiance against neutrality. You are an Overcomer and have supernatural help in praying and proclaiming the gospel where God has placed you.

After reading this chapter, I encourage you to set down this book and go for a walk. Take a swing at the Dragon and two beasts. It's really that simple.

BABYLON HAS FALLEN

The second of three angels is also proclaiming the gospel, but from a different angle, and I think we should pay special attention to it. In Revelation 14:8, we read, "Another angel, a second, followed, saying, 'Fallen, fallen is Babylon the great, she who made all nations drink the wine of the passion of her sexual immorality.'"

We need to remember that this angel isn't speaking to a literal Babylon. Physical Babylon disappeared forever in a previous judgment from God and will never rise again (Jeremiah 50:39–40; 51:26, 64; Isaiah 13:19–22). This is a reference to the conflict between spiritual Babylon and the church.

The angel flies directly overhead between heaven and earth and proclaims that Babylon has fallen. This is so important to us as Overcomers as we're seeing it right before our eyes. As this angel flies, he proclaims among those lost and far from God that their way of life is bankrupt and broken. Although the media and other outlets have us believing that people hate us as Christians, I'm personally running into very little of that. I'm having conversations about the brokenness of our culture right now weekly.

As I'm writing this chapter, in the past week there have been two mass shootings committed by eighteen-year-olds. The United States is as divided as it's been in sixty years, and the news is filled with wave after wave of disease, conflict, or some perverse view of reality.

Humankind is meant to dwell in the presence of God. Where that is, the predominant posture of humanity flourishes; but the further we move from this, the more sexually perverse and violent we become. The brokenness and perversion of our day is leading people to ask deeper and more spiritual questions.

As Overcomers, we need to be prepared to give them a real answer.

The second beast will be quick to give the answer of a political party or ideology. This is a false hope that actually leads to greater violence and perversion, not less.

Our culture in the West is deeply sick, sexually perverse, and comfortable with violence and gore at a level that would shock us if we weren't so immersed in it. We're dealing with a massive mental health pandemic, and our suicide rates have shot through the roof. According to the American Foundation of Suicide Prevention, 1.2 million people attempted to take their lives in 2020. Almost 46,000 of them were successful.[3] We're an anxious, depressed, and angry culture that's consistently provoked into outrage and robbed of peace.

We are lonely, angry, and lost.

The sexual revolution left us with broken homes, fragile identities, and no real way forward. The current debates about government reach, gender, and race have left people looking for deep and meaningful answers.

Luke 15 holds one of the more beautiful sentences in the Bible. Speaking of the prodigal son, who had destroyed his life pursuing Babylon, we read, "When he came to his senses" (v. 17 NIV). When he woke up, he was determined to rise and go to his father.

Here's where we come in as men and women who wake up to the reality that Babylon has fallen. As Overcomers, we proclaim the good news to those who are shaken out of their slumber by the brokenness of this world.

When our friends and coworkers mourn the world's brokenness, we agree with them that it's broken and take the opportunity to share ultimate hope: That justice will prevail, and wrongs will be made right. That mourning will turn into dancing, and beauty will be born from ashes.

As testimonies are given in the baptistry of the church I pastor, I hear this story over and over again: Something of Babylon's bankruptcy is quickened in a neighbor, friend, or family member, and they wake up to their way of life not working. In proximity to them is their Christian friend uniquely designed by God and placed by God so men might seek Him and find Him, though He is not far from any of them (Acts 17:26–27).

You are that friend. You are in proximity. You have supernatural help.

It's been given to you to help those who are far from God as they wake up to the bankruptcy of Babylon.

WRATH AND REPENTANCE

The third and final angel came not proclaiming that those who dwell on earth should worship him who made heaven and earth or that Babylon has fallen. This third angel proclaimed God's just, right wrath against those who worship the beast. Revelation 14:9–11 says:

> And another angel, a third, followed them, saying with a loud voice, "If anyone worships the beast and its image and receives a mark on his forehead or on his hand, he also will drink the wine of God's wrath, poured full strength into the cup of his anger, and he will be tormented with fire and sulfur in the presence of the holy angels and in the presence of the Lamb. And the smoke of their torment goes up forever and ever, and they have no rest, day or night, these worshipers of the beast and its image, and whoever receives the mark of its name."

Not long after my conversion, I knew two main points of Christian doctrine: Jesus saves, and those who reject His offer of salvation will go to hell. This became my method of evangelism. I'd share Jesus' love and grace first, and where that was rejected, I'd move to the reality of hell.

Jimmy Herford sat behind me in my US history class the year after I became a Christian. He was at a table with me in the high school library when I shared the gospel with a group of friends and then answered their questions about what exactly that meant for my sex life and the party scene. Later on, I handed him a tract to read in class. Jimmy let me know he'd love to give his life to Jesus, but he listed all the ways he was walking in sin and felt as though he couldn't be a Christian.

A few days later in class I pulled a cinnamon Jolly Rancher out of my pocket and popped it into my mouth. Jimmy leaned forward and asked for a piece. I handed him one, and he gave it back to me informing me that he didn't like fire—that's what cinnamon Jolly Ranchers are called.

Now, I tell this story to my shame, and I'm sure it violates every rule of friendship evangelism out there. But I was new to my faith and zealous for the name of Jesus, and I responded to Jimmy by telling him if he didn't like fire, he had better think seriously about what I'd been sharing.

Jimmy and I laugh about this story now, but at the time, he was far from God, and the idea of God's wrath and hell shook Jimmy. It wasn't long after that, on a Wednesday night at First Baptist Church of Texas City, that Jimmy gave his life to Jesus and is following Him to this day.

I know the idea of God having wrath and "the smoke of their torment [going] up forever and ever" has led quite a few people to wrestle with their faith. It's a terrible sentence for sure, yet as we have already covered, God has wrath because He *is* love.

Following the Dragon and the beasts is to participate in the destruction of human flourishing; the deception and destruction of men, women, and children; and the worshiping of political ideology and power. It is zeal given to false religion and the disruption and destruction of the shalom that God designed the universe to operate in. What kind of God would He be if He didn't have wrath toward that? You don't want an indifferent God. An indifferent God is far crueler than what we just read in these passages.

The second thing to consider here is when the Bible talks about God and wrath, it always frames it as giving humankind what they want. In John 3:19, we read: "And this is the judgment: the light has come into the world, and people loved the darkness rather than the light because their works were evil."

What's the judgment? Christ has come into the world to give Himself so that we might be saved from condemnation. Christ has come not to judge the world but to save the world from condemnation. He hasn't come to condemn the people we know and love; He has come to save them from condemnation.

It's people who love darkness rather than the light, so God gives them what they want. We see this again in Romans 1:28, where Paul wrote, "And since they did not see fit to acknowledge God, God gave them up to a debased mind to do what ought not to be done."

People refuse to acknowledge God. They want to be their own god, they want to follow the Dragon and his beasts, so God gives them what they want. J. I. Packer said it this way:

> Nobody stands under the wrath of God except those who have chosen to do so. The essence of God's action in wrath is to give men what they choose in all its implications: nothing more and, equally, nothing less.[4]

Let's not lose sight of what's happening here. We have supernatural help in the supernatural act of telling people the good news of salvation. Like the other two angels who come proclaiming, this angel, too, lifts eyes and ears to Jesus enthroned and on high. This angel, too, helps the church in the Great Commission to tell to the ends of the earth that a Savior has come and defeated sin and death forever.

Of the three angelic proclamations, this is the one I go to the least. It's not that it isn't true, but it takes some relational fortitude to share the gospel in our day through the lens of God's wrath. There are a lot of contextual hurdles to overcome.

With that said, I still, to this day, will move a conversation with others about faith to this end. These three angels go with us into the plentiful harvest that Jesus promised. The harvest is expansive and goes from our neighborhoods to the nations.

ENOUGH FOR US ALL

The next scene in Revelation 14 is that of two harvests. The first is mentioned in verses 14–16:

> Then I looked, and behold, a white cloud, and seated on the cloud one like a son of man, with a golden crown on his head, and a sharp sickle in his hand. And another angel came out of the temple, calling with a loud voice to him who sat on the cloud, "Put in your sickle, and reap, for the hour to reap has come, for the harvest of the earth is fully ripe." So he who sat on the cloud swung his sickle across the earth, and the earth was reaped.

The question I want to answer is: When are these harvests? Is this a reference to some future end-time harvest? I don't think so. In John 4:35 and Luke 10:2, Jesus taught that the fields were white and fully ripe for harvest. This was said not at the crucifixion or resurrection, but in both instances, Jesus spoke these words near the beginning of His ministry.

Revelation isn't a linear book. With your own eyes you've watched men, women, and children surrender to Jesus upon hearing of His glory and goodness. You've marveled as friends and family members realized life wasn't working and called on the name of Jesus, and you've watched people move out from under God's wrath and into His mercy and grace. We're reading about the great harvest of the church age, that time between Jesus' birth and the ultimate renewal of all things at His return.

In this first harvest, we see Jesus harvesting from every tribe, tongue, and nation on earth. It's important to note that Jesus didn't die on the cross for people who might be saved but for those who will be saved. This is what should embolden our evangelism. He's purchased with His blood men and women from every tribe, tongue, and nation on earth. We get to participate in that with divine help. This is the first harvest—Jesus on the cloud, sickle in His hand, swings it down because it's ripe for harvest.

We participate in the great call to make war against the Dragon and his beasts. We become a real problem for the powers and princi- palities by faithfully joining with these angels and this harvest.

The second harvest is more complex, and I hold a bit of a minority position on it. Revelation 14:17–20 says:

> Then another angel came out of the temple in heaven, and he too had a sharp sickle. And another angel came out from the altar, the angel who has authority over the fire, and he called with a loud voice to the one who had the sharp sickle, "Put in your sickle and gather the clusters from the vine of the earth, for its grapes are ripe." So the angel swung his sickle across the earth and gathered the grape harvest of the earth and threw it into the great winepress of the

wrath of God. And the winepress was trodden outside the city, and blood flowed from the winepress, as high as a horse's bridle, for 1,600 stadia.

This reads like the stuff of nightmares, and most scholars think this is the corresponding harvest of those who have rejected God and worshiped the Dragon. They may be right, but I think there's something potentially beautiful in what's happening here. It was pastor and theologian Darrell Johnson who first drew my attention to this gruesome scene with fresh eyes.[5]

First, this isn't Jesus swinging the sickle. He swung the first one. This is an angel and the angel who has authority over fire. What does fire represent nine times out of ten in the Scriptures? The presence and power of God. Was it not through a burning bush not being consumed that Moses heard from the Lord and delivered God's people out of slavery? Was it not through a pillar of fire that God led His people through the desert into the promised land? Was it not tongues of fire that fell on top of the apostles, breaking loose the Holy Spirit on the church of Jesus Christ? This angel has authority over fire, over presence, and over power.

The second thing to notice is that the harvest is "the vine of the earth" (v. 18). That phrase is mentioned six other places in the Scriptures, and it always references the people of God. In John 15:5, Jesus said, "I am the vine; you are the branches. Whoever abides in me and I in him, he it is that bears much fruit."

Lastly, you see the phrase "outside the city" (v. 20). Here's what is going to happen. When all things are said and done, there's definitely an "outside the city" that you don't want to be in. That's the wrath of God. Those who have chosen the wrath of God will be outside the city. In fact, some pretty graphic language is used there. They're trying to get in, and they cannot.

The phrase "outside the city" is used in various ways in the Scriptures. Certainly in the book of Leviticus and Numbers, "outside the camp" is a negative. It's unclean out there. You go to the bathroom out there. You kick people out there who have defiled a holy and living God.

But by the time we get to the New Testament and, specifically, when we get to first-century preaching, this idea is starting to shift. It's starting to change. Jesus told the parable of the son of the vineyard owner who was killed outside the city. Jesus was crucified outside the city. In Hebrews 13:12–13, there's the reminder that Jesus was crucified outside the camp and we should join Him there. I think what we're seeing in this harvest is Jesus Christ on the cross with the wrath of God's winepress being poured onto Him, which is why He's not the one swinging the sickle. Instead, He's absorbing all of God's wrath for those who would believe, those past, present, and future.

This is a minority view, but I think it fits with the whole of Scripture and it's beautiful in light of the rest of the chapter. Even the grotesque picture of blood has a message of hope. According to this passage, the blood was as high as a horse's bridle. Horses vary in breed and size, but on average that's four feet. The winepress of God's wrath produced four feet of blood across 1,600 stadia, which is roughly 200 miles—the length of ancient Palestine. That's an incredible amount of blood.

What is this communicating to first-century followers of Jesus Christ and to us today? There's enough blood to cleanse you from all unrighteousness. Christ's death on the cross has fully absorbed God's wrath toward you—you are free. You are clean. You have right standing before God. You're no longer condemned but delighted in.

This would've energized the saints of God, not terrified them. Jesus isn't trying to terrify His church. He's trying to say, again in a different and more vibrant way, "I have you. You're Mine! You are secure in My love. You have not screwed up beyond repair. You have not outpaced My forgiveness. You will not sit under My wrath. Look at how much blood there is. There's enough for all who would repent and believe in My name."

This shouldn't be terrifying. This should be worship-inducing. The great winepress of God's wrath? Absolutely. Where was it poured out? On Jesus so that it could be said of us that we're no longer under wrath but under mercy.

There's no sin with more power than the cross of Christ and no one you know who is so hardened that God cannot save them. Isaiah was right when he said the arms of the Lord are not too short to save (59:1).

God doesn't have T-Rex arms. Prayer walk your neighborhoods, open your dinner tables, and pray. You have supernatural help in heralding the good news. Overcomers aren't neutral in the cosmic battle. We're on the front lines armed with the Holy Spirit and angels from on high.

This whole chapter is bookended by the redeemed saints across all space and time. In Revelation 14:1–5, there we are—every tribe, tongue, and nation on earth. We're singing and making war. Then, in verse 15, right before you get to the bowls of God's wrath, you see it again: people from every tribe, tongue, and nation on earth, the army of the Lamb 144,000 strong.

Remember, 144,000 is the number of completeness. All of us are there. One of my favorite theologians encouraged us by what we see there:

The new Israel of God is made up of Jews and Gentiles, Jews and Arabs and Kenyans and Norwegians and Brazilians and Japanese, multi-cultural, multi-lingual, multi-racial, and transnational. They are all there with the King ready to sing a new song. Currently spread across the globe this is hard for us to see but it's real and you're a key part of it.[6]

Although Revelation 15–16 are disturbing chapters to examine, I believe they are significant and can offer encouragement. The imagery is meant to help us understand hard realities. Revelation also repeats themes to reinforce ideas. The number seven is used again and again. Each time events bring about blood, death, and disaster, they are followed by Overcomers gathered in worship. We've already witnessed the seals and trumpets, and now we observe the bowls of wrath. Like the trumpets, these bowls affect the earth, seas, rivers, sun, pit and throne of evil, and river Euphrates. I argue that these seven bowls represent a picture of now, viewed from Jesus' throne. From His perspective the story of redemption looks much different from ours here on earth. His commands are meant for our good, and even at our best, there is a chasm between us and a holy God. As we better understand this, our eyes are opened to God's patient compassion. We discover that God's wrath is not rage but His holiness revealed. As Overcomers, we have assurance that God's wrath toward us was fully absorbed by Jesus' death on the cross. We are now free to experience His mercy. I finish the chapter by looking at Revelation 17–18 and the seduction of Babylon before evil turns on itself and Babylon is destroyed by the beast. She is exposed and emptied of blessings. I challenge you to consider how we respond to Babylon.

CHAPTER 10

HOLINESS DOESN'T PLAY

Before becoming a Christian, I had a couple of go-to arguments if you wanted to talk to me about Jesus, whom I had no intention of following. It's not lost on me that this makes the direction of my life ironic.

If someone brought up God or Jesus, I'd simply bring up evil and suffering. I'd ask them to help me understand how God could be loving and the world could be so broken. I'd highlight whatever recent heinous act of man or natural disaster had taken place as my illustration.

A couple of times, people would attempt to answer. From there, I'd move to God's wrath, hell, and eternal damnation. I asked Jeff Faircloth, the guy who was instrumental in my becoming a Christian, this very question. I asked Jeff, If I was guilty of only a single white lie, would that be enough to damn me forever?

To me, this was an ace of spades. What could he say? If he said yes, then the punishment doesn't fit the crime to any reasonable thinker, and if he said no, then he doesn't believe his Bible—or at least my understanding of it at the time. Jeff's response was to ask me if that's all I thought I was guilty of. He always refused to play the hypothetical game with me. At some level, these were my objections to Jesus.

If we're honest, there are some difficult passages, grotesque images, and disturbing commands in the Scriptures. Revelation 15–16 might be ground zero for grotesque and violent imagery. Before studying them more carefully, I wondered if these chapters needed to be in the Bible. I wasn't sure how they helped anyone, Christian or not. If we weren't so used to violent images, these two chapters might make us nauseous.

As we did back in chapter 6, we need to look straight into these grotesque images, understand them, and let them shape and form us in real ways. Later in this chapter, we'll look at the pull of culture on us as Overcomers, and we'll need the imagery of Revelation 15–16 to help us walk through the seduction we see in chapter 17. I pray that by the end of this chapter, you'll be encouraged at the mercies of God that are new every morning and still feel the weight of God's holiness along with what that means for a world in league with the Dragon and his two beasts.

We won't be able to understand these two chapters without going back and reminding ourselves of some things we learned in chapter 2. The first is that Revelation jumps around. It's a series of windows, not a linear unfolding of a story. We saw that in chapter 7 as we got a very different picture of Christmas morning told in the present tense. The birth of Jesus took place close to ninety years before this was written, but John told us the story as if it followed what he had just written. Revelation isn't a linear unfolding of a story, and that's not normally true about other books of the Bible. As we have seen, Revelation is apocalyptic in its genre and, therefore, has unique rules. If it's talking about a future event, it'll clearly state that it is—like in several of the prophecies found in Daniel.

The second thing to remember is the imagery given to us in the book of Revelation is meant to hook us and draw us into realities that are hard for us to understand without the images. If I were to say to you, "The devil is out to destroy you," you might just start thinking of some cartoonish character with a little red cape and a pitchfork. Apocalyptic literature like Revelation wants us to feel something as much as it wants us to know something.

The question isn't, Is Satan an actual dragon? No. He's not an actual dragon, but he's an actual being. How should we think of him? Like a ferocious dragon we're locked in combat with.

How are we to think about the demonically informed state and religious institutions of our day that teach false religion? We're to think of them as two beasts sent to devour the people of God. They're not literal beasts. We're to think of them as beasts: ugly, powerful, evil, sinister, and bent on destroying us and the works of God. This provokes in us what is most true and invites us into the story we're living in.

This brings us to Revelation 15–16. Are there really seven angels with seven bowls of wrath, or is God wanting to provoke something in us at a deeper level than just knowing some facts?

RECAPITULATION

Lauren and I have decided there will be no TVs in bedrooms in our home. There are a variety of reasons for this. Some are spiritual, and others are simply practical. One practical reason is Lauren can fall asleep with the television on and I cannot. This can be problematic when we're in a hotel together. Lauren likes to turn something on to fall asleep to, and she does—usually in about fifteen minutes.

For some reason, I get sucked into the story being told, and I need some kind of resolution, so I can't sleep and I find myself unable to turn it off. What makes this even dumber is it can happen watching movies I've seen dozens of times. I'm in trouble if we come across *Saving Private Ryan, Braveheart, Gladiator, About Time,* or *The Godfather.* I've watched each many times, yet I still get sucked in and will watch into the wee hours of the morning.

Recently, we were on vacation and flipping through the channels when we landed on *Groundhog Day* with Bill Murray and Andie MacDowell. I've watched this movie more times than I can count. Lauren was excited to "watch it" and was in REM sleep fifteen minutes later. I watched as cynical weatherman Phil Connors lives the same day over and over and over again in Punxsutawney, Pennsylvania. Each day is the same but slightly different as Phil tries to escape February 2. *Groundhog Day* repeatedly shows us the same day with nuance to draw out a point it's trying to make. This is called recapitulation.

Recapitulation is a literary device where the main point or moral of the story is retold or restated to create continuity and effect. The Bible uses this literary device frequently. It's most visible in Jesus following Israel's journey from slavery to salvation. Jesus came out of Egypt (Matthew 2) like Israel did, He was baptized in the Jordan River, where Israel crossed into the promised land (Matthew 3), and He spent forty days in the wilderness like Israel spent forty years in the wilderness (Matthew 4). But, unlike Israel, Jesus was faithful at each point. The life of Jesus is a recapitulation of the story of creation, the story of God's people. Where Israel failed, Jesus succeeded and imputed that success to us as His sons and daughters.

The book of Revelation has been doing this to us since we started. We just needed to get deeper in before we could see it. There are seven seals, seven trumpets, and seven bowls. Three sevens. We already know from our study that seven is the perfect number. It means complete, and three sevens mean completely complete. As we see these three events, each is filled with blood, death, and natural calamity, and each is followed by a picture of the Overcomers gathered before Jesus in worship.

Is your mind spinning? Mine was when I first noticed this. We've already witnessed two sections of Revelation where it appears we've reached the climax only to see it all kick up again.

In Revelation 8:1, after the seventh seal is opened, there's silence in heaven, and all the prayers of the saints are brought before God. There's this scene of worship across all time and space where the people of God have been gathered before His throne. When you read this, it looks like the pinnacle, the ending, our great victory—but the story swings to the seven trumpets.

Then in Revelation 11:15, we read, "Then the seventh angel blew his trumpet, and there were loud voices in heaven, saying, 'The kingdom of the world has become the kingdom of our Lord and of his Christ, and he shall reign forever and ever.'"

That sounds like the ending of the book, but it's not. It goes from that into the interlude and introduces us to the Dragon. Then we see the woman and the beasts, and then the story shows us this mighty and vast army that we are part of.

That brings us to Revelation 15–16 and the bowls of wrath. This is recapitulation. The passages are trying to get us to feel something at a deeper level than just facts. What are these grotesque images of painful sores, the oceans and rivers turning to blood, the sun scorching humanity, darkness overcoming the earth, and three unclean spirits that rally the enemies of God together meant to provoke in us? The same thing the seven seals and seven trumpets provoked in us: the holiness and righteousness of God is ultimate reality and never to be played with.

All three "sevens" (seals, trumpets, bowls) are the same event from differing perspectives. We're seeing recapitulation. If you read the seven bowls of God's wrath and the seven trumpets, you're going to find they line up almost identically—not completely (there's nuance in some imagery), but they line up. They are very, very similar.

The first trumpet affects the earth. The first trumpet is blown, and hail, blood, and fire fall on the earth and kill hundreds of thousands if not millions of people. Now, remember, this is imagery. That doesn't mean we go outside and look around for hail, blood, and fire to come down. It's the wrath of God made visible.

Then, when we look at the bowls of God's wrath, the first bowl is poured out on the earth, and sores cover the bodies of men and women. Both the first trumpet and the first bowl affect life on the earth. The second trumpet and bowl affect the seas. The third trumpet and bowl affect the rivers. The fourth trumpet and bowl affect the sun. The fifth trumpet affects the pit of evil, and the fifth bowl affects the throne of evil. The sixth trumpet and bowl affect the river Euphrates.

Again, remember, this is imagery. This isn't saying we actually look at the sun and it's blotted out or turns to blood. What does the sun give to and provide humanity? That is what starts to be taken from it. The seven seals are the story of redemption to humankind rebelling against God, and God pursuing us to call us back into right relationship. The seven seals are the story of redemption seen from the perspective of a suffering church.

In the seven trumpets, we see that same thing. People rebel against God, and God pursues them to pull them back into His created purpose from the perspective of sinful men and women. Then, here, in the seven bowls, we're seeing the story of redemption from the perspective of the throne of Jesus. Each of these images is a picture of the church age between the birth of Jesus and His ultimate return. They're not in the future. They are now.

This doesn't change anything about how horrific these two chapters are. So we're back staring at God's wrath, and we're forced to come to grips with it. We've covered quite a bit of this already, but let's look at two more things before we look at our ultimate victory and our future glory.

CRUEL AND UNUSUAL?

George Mason was an American politician and founding father. Along with Edmund Randolph of Virginia and Elbridge Gerry of Massachusetts, he refused to sign the Constitution as it was written. Mason had written a pamphlet against the new government that persuaded people to oppose the new government. Mason argued that the Constitution as it was written wouldn't protect the people from government overreach and tyranny.

This led James Madison to write amendments to the Constitution and "hound his colleagues relentlessly" to secure its passage. These amendments became known as the Bill of Rights and focused on what the founding fathers considered inalienable rights, sometimes called "natural laws."[1]

According to Richard Foltin of the Freedom Forum, an inalienable right is "a right that can't be restrained or repealed by human laws."[2] For example, the Eighth Amendment outlaws government's use of "cruel and unusual punishment." Punishment needs to fit the crime.

One of the main issues people will raise about God's wrath is it violates this natural law. This is a matter of perspective more than reality. Revelation 15:5 places us in a location where we can see things a little differently. It says, "After this I looked, and the sanctuary of the tent of witness in heaven was opened." The perspective of human history we're reading isn't one of the church or those far from God. It's from the "sanctuary of the tent of witness." We've read about this place before in Numbers 1. It's that place in the tabernacle by which the presence and the moral law of God exist. We see the bowls of wrath from the perspective of the holiness of God, the presence of God, and the moral commands of God that are meant to lead to human flourishing rather than human destruction.

From this perspective, everything changes. If I look at myself and others on a horizontal plane and compare the best people to the worst people, I can look really good, and so can the bulk of humanity. This is how most people decide that 90 percent of humans are simply good people doing the best they can.

But things unravel quickly if the comparison is between us and a holy God. Everyone in the Bible who comes across an angel and their holiness, which is nothing but a tiny reflection of God's holiness, falls on the ground as if they're about to be consumed. There's no swagger in the presence of God. His holiness decimates and destroys anything that's unrighteous.

Isaiah 64:6 lets us know that all our good deeds and righteousness, all those ways we consider ourselves good people, are like a "polluted garment":

> We have all become like one who is unclean,
> and all our righteous deeds are like a polluted garment.
> We all fade like a leaf,
> and our iniquities, like the wind, take us away.

What makes this true isn't discovered by comparing ourselves to others and trying to measure ourselves over and above friends and family members. God's white-hot, fierce holiness exposes this and destroys anything that's not perfect.

The Bible says when Jesus returns, the mountains will flee before

Him, the elements will dissolve, and the earth will melt like wax. What's happening? His holiness is chasing out and decimating anything that has been touched by sin, any perverse residue, anything that's less than perfect, and anything that refuses to acknowledge His holiness or wants something other than His presence. That's God's perspective on redemptive history, and it's full of His long-suffering compassion.

Wrath is coming forth from this place because people think they're a better god than God in thousands of ways every day, leading to immense human suffering. When I think back to the argument I tried to make with Jeff, I was really saying, "I know how the universe should work better than God does."

Romans 1:18–20 says:

> The wrath of God is being revealed from heaven against all the godlessness and wickedness of people, who suppress the truth by their wickedness, since what may be known about God is plain to them, because God has made it plain to them. For since the creation of the world God's invisible qualities—his eternal power and divine nature—have been clearly seen, being understood from what has been made, so that people are without excuse.

This is saying you don't have to grow up in church to know there's something divine. You don't have to grow up in church to know there's a right and wrong and there's a God. By nature of being human, we feel shame, guilt, despair, and longing—a kind of soul-level angst that there's something more out there, a law to be obeyed, a God to know. God has made Himself known, and humankind has said, "No, thank you."

Romans 1 says we begin to suppress both our shame and the longing. We squash it. God's response to this has been to pursue humanity across every nook and cranny on the globe to call them into His perfection and holiness, to call them out from under the destruction that will come when the full weight of His glory is revealed.

John 3:19 says, "And this is the judgment: the light has come into the world, and people loved the darkness rather than the light because their works were evil." Do you want to understand judgment and God's wrath? John laid it out: God sent light into the world, gave humankind the "path of life" (Psalm 16:11) in His moral law for human flourishing, and then sent Jesus into the world to save us from the weight of His glory and holiness. Yet people refuse it and choose to be their own gods, causing unthinkable destruction on God's creation and other people.

When we think of wrath, we tend to think of rage, but God is holy and perfect. He sees all of us rebel, suppress, and reject while destroying His creation, and He doesn't respond with wrath or malice. His wrath is His holiness revealed. God's wrath isn't rage.

Theologian Thomas F. Torrance said it like this:

> The wrath which [the angels] are about to pour out upon the earth is a pure and sinless wrath, priestly in its function and golden in its integrity. . . no bestial passion, no spite, no hate, no anger of sin at all in it. The holiness of God just destroying anything that is not protected by the blood of Jesus.[3]

THE RING

Before J. R. R. Tolkien's brilliant Lord of the Rings trilogy, we're introduced to a hideous creature named Gollum in his book *The Hobbit*. He's described as "a small, slimy creature" who lived on a small island in an underground lake at the roots of the Misty Mountains. He survived on cave fish, which he caught from a small boat, and small goblins who strayed too far from the stronghold of the Great Goblin. Over the years, Gollum's eyes adapted to the dark and became "lamp-like," shining with a sickly pale light.[4]

Gollum wasn't always a grotesque and evil creature. He was originally named Sméagol and had once been a member of the secluded branch of the early Stoorish Hobbits. He spent the early years of his life with his extended family under a matriarch, his grandmother.

Upon finding the Ring on his birthday, he immediately falls under the Ring's influence and murders his friend Déagol. This begins centuries of being tormented and deformed by the Ring. Gollum "loved and hated [the Ring], as he loved and hated himself."[5]

Throughout Tolkien's story, Gollum is torn between his lust for the Ring and his desire to be free of it. Ultimately, Gollum's death is wrapped up in the Ring's destruction. As the Ring falls to its demise in the fires of Mount Doom, so does Gollum as he chases it with his very last breath. The fires of Mount Doom weren't for Gollum; they were for the Ring. Despite all the pain, torment, and loss, he couldn't let go of it.

Similarly, sin twists humanity and leads us to fires that weren't created for us but for Satan and his angels (Matthew 25:41). The wrath of God is aimed primarily at the Dragon and the beasts. When people repeatedly choose to sidle up to the Dragon, they get caught up in the wrath meant for the Dragon. The choice people make when they suppress the truth and choose darkness over the light is to join the Dragon and beasts in their future. It's horrific and heartbreaking.

If you want to see humanity's wickedness from God's perspective, look at Revelation 16. Three times in this chapter—in verses 9, 11, and 21—it says the people experiencing the result of the brokenness of the fall curse, blame, and accuse God of being the author by which this brokenness comes. They curse God, but it's God who has conquered the Dragon and the beast. God brings light, but people love the darkness. God brings real life, but people choose spiritual death. God brings care for the poor and marginalized but gets blamed for oppression. God brings liberty but is blamed for bondage. God gives the good gifts of food, sex, community, money, and play but is mocked and belittled by His creation concerning His instructions.

Humankind's accusations reveal their wickedness.

As Overcomers, we feel the weight of this. We see people trapped, like Gollum, who can't or won't let go of the Dragon. That's why we can't be neutral, shrink back, or be silent. That's why we must say something when our friends blame a holy God for the things the Dragon and his henchmen author.

THE GOOD NEWS!

Unlike God's love, His wrath has an expiration date. The wrath of God will eventually be finished forever. Remember, God *is* love (1 John 4:8). That will never change. Sixty trillion years from now, the triune God of the Bible will be perfect in love, lavishing that love on His adopted sons and daughters who through faith and grace alone have come into His kingdom out from under wrath and into His mercy.

Look at Revelation 15:1: "Then I saw another sign in heaven, great and amazing, seven angels with seven plagues, which are the last, for with them the wrath of God is finished." The wrath of God is finished, so His love remains, and His wrath is over.

Now look at Revelation 16:17: "The seventh angel poured out his bowl into the air." Who is the "prince of the power of the air" (Ephesians 2:2)? Satan and his angels. "And a loud voice came out of the temple, from the throne, saying, 'It is done!'" This is showing the final outcome of Jesus' life, death, and resurrection.

This isn't the first time we've seen the phrase "it is done" in the Bible. We heard it from Jesus' very lips on the cross:

> After this, Jesus, knowing that all was now finished, said (to fulfill the Scripture), "I thirst." A jar full of sour wine stood there, so they put a sponge full of the sour wine on a hyssop branch and held it to his mouth. When Jesus had received the sour wine, he said, "It is finished," and he bowed his head and gave up his spirit. (John 19:28–30)

John put an echo in this for the people of God: those who were the people of God in AD 96 and those who are going to become the people of God and read these words after. These words are here for you.

If you're a Christian, if you can be an Overcomer, the wrath of God is spent. It's been fully absorbed by the death of Jesus on the cross. You are now under mercy.

One of the harder parts of being a pastor is to see the sheer volume of people who still live their Christian lives as though they're under the wrath of God when the Bible is clear that when you wake up in the morning, what's waiting for you is enough mercy for each day.

Wouldn't it be great to finally just believe: "God knows, and He's got me. I'm secure, so let me walk as faithfully as I can today with where I am, leaning into His grace and presence?" In other words, if you would ever get it in your head that you're not under wrath, but the banner over your life is love and God is pleased with you, loves you, and delights in you, you would walk more powerfully as an Overcomer.

Refuse to believe that God is perpetually angry at you. You're not under wrath; you're under mercy. You might get disciplined because He is a good Father, but any difficulty in your life is never His wrath. The Bible says you are under mercy.

When we talk about victory, prayerfulness, worship, and presence, we talk about things that have been given to you by grace. These things are yours to pick up.

As Overcomers, we understand that God's wrath is rooted in His holiness and the weight of His glory. He desires that all men be saved and that none should perish. It's not rage; it's pure priestly fire. To see this and understand it is of the utmost importance for the Overcomer.

SHE TURNS MEN TO STONE

In Greek mythology, Medusa was a stunningly beautiful woman who drew the eye of the god Poseidon, who assaulted her in Athena's temple. Athena, powerless to exact revenge on Poseidon, took out her anger on Medusa by turning her beautiful hair into snakes and her beautiful legs into a serpent's body. To make matters worse, Athena cursed Medusa so anyone who looked upon her would be instantly turned to stone.

In Revelation, we see a similar and more hideous creature who seduces men and women and then devours them. Revelation 17:1–6 says:

> Then one of the seven angels who had the seven bowls came and said to me, "Come, I will show you the judgment of the great prostitute who is seated on many waters, with whom the kings of the earth have committed sexual immorality, and with the wine of whose sexual immorality the dwellers on earth have become drunk." And he carried me away in the Spirit into a wilderness, and I saw a woman sitting on a scarlet beast that was full of blasphemous names, and it had seven heads and ten horns. The woman was arrayed in purple and scarlet, and adorned with gold and jewels and pearls, holding

in her hand a golden cup full of abominations and the impurities of her sexual immorality. And on her forehead was written a name of mystery: "Babylon the great, mother of prostitutes and of earth's abominations." And I saw the woman, drunk with the blood of the saints, the blood of the martyrs of Jesus.

This passage is filled with wild imagery. We have a prostitute riding the first beast, which was mentioned in Revelation 13. Remember, the beast this prostitute is riding represents the state that seeks to move our affection and worship off Jesus and put it on governmental structures and systems.

The name on her forehead is significant. Things written on foreheads in Revelation are a symbol of ideology. On hers it says, "Babylon the great, mother of prostitutes and of earth's abominations" (17:5). The image of the prostitute is the right image for what we're dealing with here. She is lewd, yet we can't take our eyes off her. We know it's wrong, yet we're drawn toward her.

She represents the city of man. She represents what humankind can build in rebellion against God. This imagery is a picture of a human city that exalts itself as divine rather than submitting to the King of kings and Lord of lords. That's the picture we're getting.

She's on the back of the beast, and she's beautiful. She's so beautiful that in Revelation 17:6–7 we see John admit, "When I saw her, I marveled greatly. But the angel said to me, 'Why do you marvel? I will tell you the mystery of the woman, and of the beast with seven heads and ten horns that carries her.'" Even John gets sucked in by her beauty and has to be rebuked by the angel.

Here's a warning to the church: culture is a seductress, and she's better at it than most of us think.

If the apostle whom Jesus loved, who rested his head on Christ's chest at the Last Supper, can look at her and marvel, we can get sucked up in it too. This is a word of warning to the church for right now, and we're caught in it. She's on the back of that beast, and she's calling, "This is the way to life. This is the way to meaning. This is where you'll be free. This is where you'll have comfort. This is where you'll be wealthy."

John warned us, "Watch out for her. She's prettier than you think she is. Watch out for her. She'll seduce you. Be careful. You'll feel like you've got it, and you'll just take one look at her, and be turned to stone."

BABYLON'S SEDUCTION

To shake us out of the seductress's stare, the angel shows us what she really is. Babylon is the promise of any great city embedded into any great nation that tries to woo people away from God, and it's always a bait and switch. The prostitute is promising power, opulence, comfort, wealth, and your best life. That's the promise.

She is wooing. She's even saying, "Yeah, life is hard. Do you know what would make it better? This kind of sexual sensuality. You should get into that. Do you know what would make it better? Great wealth, and I have great wealth. Serve me. Follow me. Bow to me. Worship me. I'll keep you safe. I'll make sure your life is good. I'll make sure you're happy. Jesus isn't going to make you happy. Why would you go to Him? Look how rigid His rules are. He's always trying to take from you, saying, 'Don't do *this* and don't do *this* and don't do *this*.'"

This is what the prostitute does. This is her song: "Life is found in me. Submit. Surrender. This is the way you should live." It's built on an illusion. It promises comfort and ease and sensual satisfaction, but the reality is she cannot deliver on those promises. She has no power by which to fulfill those promises.

In fact, even her beatitudes run contrary to Jesus' Beatitudes. In the Sermon on the Mount, Jesus laid out what citizens of His kingdom will become once they submit to Him. He led with "Blessed are the poor in spirit" (Matthew 5:3), but she begins with "Blessed are the wealthy and powerful."

Jesus ended His Beatitudes with "Blessed are those who are persecuted for righteousness' sake" (v. 10), and she ends with "Blessed are you when you persecute."

These are two different kingdoms with two different cultural artifacts and two different cultural value systems. They're at war with each other, and we're living in one of them. In this imagery, the angel of the Lord is saying to us, "Don't get seduced by her. She's better than you think. Don't get seduced by her. She's wooing you right now."

The ferocious holiness of God is so important for us to keep in front of us as Overcomers because Babylon always ends in violence toward the people of God.

BABYLON'S VIOLENCE

In Psalm 2, which ends with Jesus' feet on Mount Zion, we read:

> Why do the nations rage
> and the peoples plot in vain?
> The kings of the earth set themselves,
> and the rulers take counsel together,
> against the LORD and against his Anointed, saying,
> "Let us burst their bonds apart
> and cast away their cords from us." (vv. 1–3)

Why does Babylon always end in violence for the people of God? They think we're trying to rob them of life. The reason the nations rage against God and His people is because the way we live is an offense to them—first, because it calls them to something different and, second, because it shows a plausibility structure where humanity flourishes without worshiping the beast or bending the knee to this prostitute.

It's disorienting for them. We seem strange, like aliens and strangers. We're enemies of their progress toward utopia. The war we're caught up in is a game of seduction that ends in destruction, where this woman and this beast are trying to get you to stop worshiping Jesus, submitting to Jesus, exalting Jesus, and enjoying Jesus—and instead to find your comfort and purpose in temporary, hollow, and ultimately unsatisfactory things.

I can't state it more plainly than that, and some of us are caught in it right now. As Overcomers, we must keep our wits about us. Revelation helps us by showing not only the holiness of God but also how it all ends for cultures and governments that seek to seduce the people of God away from following Jesus.

In Revelation 17:16, we see that the beast turns on the prostitute and kills her. Babylon is destroyed by the beast. Evil always turns on itself.

The promises of a culture committed to abandoning God can never be fulfilled. There is no ideology that is ever fulfilled. There's no promise that's ultimately consummated. She is hollow and ultimately becomes a haunt for demons. Those who get seduced by the prostitute and give in to her enticing calls become demonized. The word is *demonized*, not *possessed*.

Think about it like a tick on a dog. Can that tick possess the dog? Absolutely not. Can it get so big that the dog gets sick and weak and ultimately dies? Yes. This is saying if you give in to Babylon and you give in to this seduction, you'll be bound. You'll be stuck. You'll have given yourself over to what's demonic, and you will, therefore, be demonized.

What we see next is Babylon's false foundations and illusions exposed. We see her emptied of blessing in Revelation 18:6–8. Then all of the people start to mourn, but they don't mourn that she's burning and in smoke. They mourn that they can no longer be wealthy and comfortable because of her, so there's no real love for Babylon. It's all usury. Nobody loves Babylon; they just want to use her. It's a sad and pathetic reality. It's "What can you do for me?" It's the opposite of the kingdom of God.

OUR RESPONSE TO BABYLON

With this reality in view, how are we now to live?

The church of Jesus Christ, both individually as saved persons and corporately as gathered local bodies of believers, is to live in a way that presents to the world around us a different plausibility structure than the one they know, see, and understand.

We reject the violence of Babylon. We're to be marked by peace with a tranquil heart that understands that despite what we might be seeing around us, Jesus is on His throne. There should be a rejection of the consumption of Babylon by living lives marked by radical generosity. Babylon is insatiable, saying, "I need more! I need more money. I need a bigger house. I need a nicer car. I need . . ." But we say, "How do I bless others generously with my money, time, gifts, and home?" We're to stand in stark contrast to the world that's insatiable.

We reject the sexual ethic of Babylon as she tries to promise that perversity will bring the soul-level satisfaction that He has designed for us. We must reject it. We ruthlessly and prayerfully fight in community against sexual perversion and happily embrace that sex has been given to a man and a woman within the confines of covenantal love so that souls are cherished and built up rather than consumed and devoured.

We reject the hate of Babylon by practicing radical hospitality. We break out our best food and drink and have those far from God around our dinner tables.

So I want to ask you a personal question: how have you been responding to Babylon? I think we tend to look away from these types of passages and prefer not to think deeply about what they say or mean. I know when I first studied them it awakened some repenting that I needed to do. What about you? Like John, have you seen Babylon and been seduced by her a bit? If so, that's okay. The fact that you are reading this book now is God, in His mercy, bringing you back into your rightful place.

With just a glance at her, we can be sucked in. Repentance is a gift that needs to be specific and actionable, so let's be mindful of what we're repenting of and what it looks like to walk in an opposite direction as we finish this chapter. Remember, the holiness of God destroys and decimates everything that isn't pure and perfect.

Return to God's mercy and live by His presence and power. Turn from the lies of "Babylon the great, mother of prostitutes and of earth's abominations" (Revelation 17:5) back into the arms of a holy and merciful God. The victory is His, and He wants to share it with you.

I'm reminded of God's grace each year when I gather with friends to celebrate the New Year. Together we nurture souls and strengthen community. In this way, God shapes His people around tables. This is shown in Revelation 19 with the marriage supper of the Lamb. Just as God's people have celebrated the Passover for centuries to remember their deliverance, this is a time of celebration and remembrance. It is a time of slowing down and feasting. In chapter 19, it tells us we come to the feast bringing nothing. Jesus invites us to join Him at this feast, and He provides the food and new clothes. As I move to chapter 20, I mention that it is one of the most debated chapters in Scripture. Though the different views agree on much, people have argued over time about what Jesus' thousand-year reign will be like. How we look at it affects how we live. But regardless of our view, Jesus is the ultimate judge, and we are on earth to love people. The strong man is bound, and we are plundering his property for Jesus. When we see the lost and broken, we share the good news of freedom in Christ.

CHAPTER 11

THE SPOILS OF VICTORY

For almost fifteen years, Lauren and I have gathered with four other couples to ring in the New Year. We started out making reservations at nice restaurants, but we quickly moved to getting together at one of our homes. Each year, the menu is set with one rule: bring the best we can afford. The best cuts of meat, the best wine, the best sides, and the best desserts. Each couple picks what they would like to bring, and we build out the day.

That's right, I said *day*. We arrive at the home we're gathering in early in the afternoon. We won't just eat together; we cook together. We slow down and savor one another's company as we put together an epic meal—a feast. We smell each dish and look forward with eager anticipation toward the evening together. There are appetizers and drinks, small plates of cheeses and cured meats. We linger, tell stories, laugh until our faces hurt, and slowly move toward the table. The table has been set beautifully. Joanna Gaines and Martha Stewart would be pleased. Fresh flowers, beautiful place settings, glassware, and more utensils than I knew existed growing up.

Once we make it to the table, our friend Josh Patterson has questions for the group. Some are silly, some are serious, but each is meant to pull out an awareness of God's good graces over the past year. Between each course, we pause. Again, our time together is meant to be slow, and the pace is important. Life moves fast in our world, and we're rebelling.

There are years where a couple has been beaten up with a difficult year and find themselves feeling thin, while another couple might be coming off one of the best years of their lives. I remember on New Year's Eve 2009, we paused near the end of dinner so I could take one of my first rounds of chemotherapy. It was a large vial of pills that had to be taken that evening. It was a sober and heavy night, but Lauren and I refused to miss the feast with the dear brothers and sisters given to us by God's grace.

After the meal, we move to a living room and we sing. Michael Bleecker leads us in worship, and we pray, and cry, and enjoy the presence of Jesus. There have been years where this night lasted until two or three in the morning.

In gathering like this, our minds are reminded of God's good grace, our souls are nurtured, and our community is strengthened as we practice for the coming feast where all things will be made new.

THE FEAST OF VICTORY

God has chosen to shape and form His people around tables. God has chosen to encourage, build up, empower, remind, and strengthen His people around meals. It's no surprise, then, that as we get to the end of Revelation and the end of all things, we see the "marriage supper of the Lamb":

> Then I heard what seemed to be the voice of a great multitude, like the roar of many waters and like the sound of mighty peals of thunder, crying out, "Hallelujah! For the Lord our God the Almighty reigns. Let us rejoice and exult and give him the glory, for the marriage of the Lamb has come, and his Bride has made herself ready; it was granted her to clothe herself with fine linen, bright and pure"—for the fine linen is the righteous deeds of the saints. And the angel said to me, "Write this: Blessed are those who are invited to the marriage supper of the Lamb." And he said to me, "These are the true words of God." (Revelation 19:6–9)

In a chapter setting up the final battle between good and evil—the vanquishing of Satan, death, and hades—we have a table, a feast, and the saints of God dressed in "fine linen, bright and pure."

If we think back on the story of God's people, a table in the presence of a soon-vanquished enemy is more recapitulation.

THE ORIGINAL FEAST

In Exodus 3, the people of God were enslaved. They were in bondage, and the current pharaoh had a growing disdain for the people of God. We read that God had seen their affliction and heard their cries and that He was coming down to deliver them (vv. 7–8). Over the next few chapters, we have a front-row seat to God's might and victory over the principalities and powers we've read so much about. What most Christians know as the ten plagues are actually the Dragon and his beasts being pounded easily into submission by our great God and

King. Each of the plagues is tied to a corresponding Egyptian god. The plague isn't just meant as judgment on the Egyptian people for their brutality but also as a message to the world that the Dragon and his two beasts are no match for the power of God.

When God turned the Nile into blood, He was exposing that the Egyptian god Hapi (or Osiris) has no real power over fertility and life. He isn't the life-giving force to be worshiped. He isn't all powerful. So trusting her is trusting in no god at all.

When God sent the frogs in the second plague, He was publicly executing the Egyptian god Heqet, the goddess of childbirth. The Egyptians had been killing the sons of the Israelites in a state-sponsored genocide—which, as we have seen, is the first beast—and God showed His might over this lesser principality and power.

In the third plague of lice or gnats, the sorcerers of Egypt were no longer able to duplicate the mighty works of God, but still they refused to surrender to the Creator of all things.

As we move through each plague, we see what we covered in the last chapter. The great prostitute Babylon, here seen as Egypt, cannot deliver on what she has promised, so she turns on herself and becomes a haunt for demons and wild animals. The places where the Egyptians had placed their hopes for comfort, wealth, and sexual satisfaction were all exposed as demonic principalities that can't deliver on their promises. The holy might of God showed up, destroying all that isn't holy.

After the ninth plague of darkness—which was a roundhouse kick to the jaw of the Egyptian sun god, Ra—the people of God were commanded to prepare a meal. This seems strange. In the midst of this cosmic battle, God told the people to get an unblemished lamb—the best they had—and prepare unleavened bread, gather bitter herbs, and dress for action.

The command was to take the lamb's blood and swipe it on the doorposts of their homes. This would allow the people of God to be spared the wrath of God's holiness as it killed the firstborn in all of Egypt from Pharaoh to the captive in the dungeon and the firstborn among the livestock (Exodus 11:4–5). God was weaving into the story of His people the gift of remembrance—remembrance of His power and the ultimate weakness of the Dragon and beasts over His rule and reign.

For the next sixteen hundred years, God's people gathered together to celebrate the Passover. As they ate the Passover meal in homes, their family ties, neighborliness, and hospitality increased. As they selected and roasted the lamb, they were reminded that God deserves our first and best and that they need not fear tyrannical governments— lambs were sacred to Egyptians. As they ate the bitter herbs, they were reminded of the slavery God had delivered them from. And the unleavened bread and dress for the Passover reminded them of the speed of their final deliverance and victory. They were commanded to leave none of it but eat the meal in haste as they plundered their enemies.

What do you think God was trying to teach His people at the table? What was He calling them into the wilderness for? Exodus says it was "to hold a feast to me." The feast that frees them from slavery is a feast over time that forms them as the people of God. They come back to it over and over and over again as they gather, anchoring themselves in their story, not getting lost in the one that's projected to them all around.

Remember, things aren't as they seem. God says at the table, "I know you. I see you. Have a seat. Get the herbs. Get the lamb. Remember the blood over the doorway. No one will triumph over you. I am your God."

THE FEAST FULFILLED

After close to sixteen hundred years of God's people observing the Passover, the Dragon was back at it with his two henchmen. This time the first beast (the state) had "resurrected" as Rome, and the second beast (religion) was manifesting in the form of the Pharisees and Sadducees. Jesus' earthly ministry was dynamic in that He was revealing the kingdom of God over all things.

Jesus' miracles were a sign of His ultimate authority. He rebuked the wind and waves, revealing that nature obeys His commands. He healed diseases, showing that the curse of sickness due to the fall in Genesis 3 was overcome in His coming. He raised the dead and defeated the demons at every turn.

It's always struck me that in movies about demonic possession, the priest or man of God is always killed, maimed, or driven out. The movies and shows that show spiritual realities almost always paint a picture of a type of dualism where both sides are equal, and technique and tactics determine the winner.

We just don't see that in Jesus' life. Every time Jesus came across a demonized person in the Gospels, the demon was terrified and worried that the time of his ultimate destruction had come. As we read about the kingdom of God being "at hand" in Jesus' ministry (Matthew 3:2), we see Him celebrate the Passover meal three times (John 2:13; 6:4; 13:1). Three times Jesus with His disciples found a lamb without blemish, gathered bitter herbs, made or purchased unleavened bread, and remembered. They remembered God's victory and power over darkness, and they remembered His promises to His people. It was during Jesus' final Passover that He revealed the final victory over the Dragon and his henchmen was at hand.

The Last Supper is recorded in all four Gospels, but Luke gave it the most attention. At this Passover meal, Jesus reoriented the meaning of the meal and introduced a new meal to be practiced "as often as you drink it" (1 Corinthians 11:25).

In Luke 22, we read:

And when the hour came, he reclined at table, and the apostles with him. And he said to them, "I have earnestly desired to eat this Passover with you before I suffer. For I tell you I will not eat it until it is fulfilled in the kingdom of God." And he took a cup, and when he had given thanks he said, "Take this, and divide it among yourselves. For I tell you that from now on I will not drink of the fruit of the vine until the kingdom of God comes." And he took bread, and when he had given thanks, he broke it and gave it to them, saying, "This is my body, which is given for you. Do this in remembrance of me." And likewise the cup after they had eaten, saying, "This cup that is poured out for you is the new covenant in my blood." (vv. 14–20)

The night before Jesus was crucified, surrounded by His enemies in Jerusalem with a traitor in His midst, He stopped and reached back to God's victory in Egypt and promised a new, final, and complete victory. He picked up the unleavened bread and passed it around. He broke it and said this meal was no longer about simply the speed of deliverance, but now it should remind them that His body was broken for them. The justice of God's holiness would be satisfied not by their bodies being broken but by His. He then took the cup, promised He would drink new wine with them when the kingdom came, and then said, "This cup that is poured out for you is the new covenant in my blood" (v. 20).

The blood of the unblemished lamb that was smeared on doorways is giving way to the blood of Jesus that justifies us before God (Romans 5:9); forgives all our sins, past, present, and future (Ephesians 1:7); cleanses us of all unrighteousness (1 John 1:7); gives us the power to overcome the enemy (Revelation 12:11); gives us a redemption that will never perish (1 Peter 1:18–19); gives us access to the presence and power of God (Hebrews 10:19–22), and much more.

You are an Overcomer, and this is your table, set by Jesus Himself as a precursor for the marriage supper of the Lamb.

This is hard for us because we aren't a culture that understands feasting. We're a culture of quick convenience. For many of us, dinner is throwing chicken nuggets in the back of the Suburban. We're built for speed, and because we don't understand feasting, we are famished. We don't understand pace and quiet and that Jesus is the host. We run ourselves ragged trying to prepare a meal for Him.

In Revelation 19, we see we don't bring anything to this feast. You don't bring the wine to this dinner; Jesus does. We don't show up with flowers, appetizers, or dessert. We don't even have to worry about what to wear. He gives us our clothes, and He dresses us like priests (v. 8). At the marriage supper of the Lamb, Jesus is pulling out a chair and saying, "Have a seat." This is the feast where we're just going to eat and eat and eat and drink and drink and drink and laugh and laugh and laugh. We're going to sit at this table.

This is what David rejoiced about in Psalm 23:5: "You prepare a table before me in the presence of my enemies." Eugene Peterson tied what we see in Revelation 19 back to Psalm 23 in a beautiful way:

> The Lord presides over a meal as a host; a war has rendered all enemies powerless to harm. Psalm 23 and Revelation 19 are companion pieces in the exposition of salvation, showing forth the two elements: rescue from the catastrophe of the shadow of death; hospitality at a table where we are made whole with the intimacies of goodness and mercy.[1]

Both the Passover and the Lord's Supper take place as Satan is thrashing about and convinced of his victory. The truth is, both tables were, as David said, prepared in the presence of our enemies.

In Psalm 23:4, David wrote, "Even though I walk through the valley of the shadow of death, I will fear no evil, for you are with me."

Why are we not going to be afraid? Because God is with us. This isn't our victory, but Jesus gives it to us. We don't win anything. Notice that David didn't say, "Though I walk through the valley of the shadow of death, I will fear no evil, because you are going to make me awesome." He said, "You are with me; your rod and your staff, they comfort me" (v. 4).

JESUS: Great job.
ME: What? I didn't do anything.
JESUS: No. Great job! You won. Victory is yours.
ME: Well, the victory is Yours, Jesus.
JESUS: No, I'm giving it to you.

Starting in verse 5, David showed us the table:

> You prepare a table before me
> in the presence of my enemies;
> you anoint my head with oil;
> my cup overflows.
> Surely goodness and mercy shall follow me
> all the days of my life. (vv. 5–6)

I love the imagery here. David was saying, "When I walk through the valley of the shadow of death, I won't fear any evil. Why? Because God is with me, and He has a rod, and He has a staff." As our enemy thrashes about and seeks to destroy and devour, we are invited to sit in the presence of Jesus.

That's the call to the Overcomers: to come and sit. The tables are showing us two things. First, we see our enemy is powerless. Second, we see the hospitality of Jesus where He feeds us goodness and mercy. Part of being an Overcomer is being convinced there's an actual presence of Jesus for us to know and walk in, to take seriously Jesus' teaching that those who hunger and thirst for righteousness will be filled (Matthew 5:6).

Overcomers walk in a kind of holy dissatisfaction and know that Jesus is an inexhaustible well. They hunger for more. They long to sit at the table.

THE PRESENT PLUNDER OF VICTORY

I changed my major to biblical studies after my sophomore year of college. The Lord had made it clear that I wouldn't study to become a wealthy lawyer with a great Sunday school class. Instead, He was calling me into vocational ministry. I'd worked briefly at a church before, as I did some school at a junior college. The combination of my youth and ignorance of how church works led to a disastrous experience. So I had wrongly believed that ministry wasn't for me and thought law might be a good fit. The Lord wasn't having it, and He hounded me through friends, opportunities, and a few prophetic words. I changed my major, lost a year of studies, and reluctantly started following God's calling on my life.

In my first year of theological training, my New Testament professor, Dr. James Shields, encouraged me to find an "ancient friend" who could anchor me in orthodox faith. He assured me that the day in which I lived would push and pull me theologically and a good "ancient friend" could anchor me and help me see clearly in the fog of my own time. A few months later, upon hearing a quote from Saint Augustine, I headed to the library to learn more about him.

Augustine of Hippo was a bishop in Northern Africa and a prolific writer. There was some griminess to him, and I liked that. Before Christ, he was a profuse partier and womanizer, and he once stole some pears even though he already had pears and wasn't going to eat them. He simply liked the feeling of stealing. Augustine became my ancient friend, and I began to work slowly through his dense writings. I think it took me a year to get through *The City of God*.

I've learned much from Augustine these past couple of decades, but one quote in particular has been blinking like a neon sign in my spirit in light of this current cultural moment. In his *Confessions*, Augustine wrote, "In essentials, unity. In non-essentials, liberty. In all things, love."[2] Augustine cared deeply about doctrine, and he wasn't known for being a third-way kind of guy, but he could also see how easily Christians might divide and devour one another.

I want to live this out boldly. I don't want to be forced into this camp or tribe or stream or whatever. I think Christians can disagree charitably about secondary issues and still see each other as brothers and sisters. I say all this because Revelation 20 is one of the more debated chapters in the whole Bible. I believe it's also a chapter that has the power to encourage and embolden us as Overcomers.

In Revelation 20, we see a thousand-year reign of Jesus Christ (v. 3). That's clear. He reigns for one thousand years. Satan, the Dragon, is bound and thrown into a pit, and Jesus is reigning on earth with His people (20:1–3). That's the imagery we're given. There are three orthodox views of this passage.

1. **Premillennialism** teaches that Christ's second coming will occur before the millennium and that he will reign for a literal one thousand years on the earth.
2. **Postmillennialism** teaches that Christ's second coming will be preceded by the millennium, a golden age of gospel blessing

on the ministry of the church. At Christ's coming there will be the general resurrection, the general judgment, followed by the creation of the new heavens and the new earth, and the eternal state.

3. **Amillennialism** teaches that there will be no literal thousand-year period of great spiritual blessing before the Lord Jesus returns, and no literal thousand-year reign of Christ on earth after His return. The thousand years are spiritualized to convey the idea of completeness or perfection and are a spiritual description of the entire period between Christ's ascension and the end of the age.

These three views agree on more than they disagree. In all three Jesus wins, Christ returns, the beast is thrown into hell forever, and the ultimate victory is Christ's.

Whoever ends up being right won't gloat in glory, and whoever is wrong won't be sad for eternity. I have dear friends I love deeply who land in very different places than I do. This isn't a gospel issue, even though I've seen some tribes try to make it one.

Why does this matter? Why can't we just agree to disagree and move on? The truth is, how we interpret this passage has massive implications for how we live the Christian life.

A BAZILLION

One of the things I miss about having small children is the laughter we enjoyed at their mispronouncing and making up words. My oldest couldn't say *hospital* to save her life, so it was "hostible." My son pronounced the word *awesome* as "awe-we-so-may." Another thing Reid did was respond to any question of how much time, candy, soda, or screen time with the number "bazillion." Whenever we would ask how many or how much of this thing or that thing, he would say "a bazillion." It was his way of saying "a lot."

In 2 Peter 3:8, the apostle Peter, quoting from Psalm 90:4, said, "But do not overlook this one fact, beloved, that with the Lord one day is as a thousand years, and a thousand years as one day."

Twice in the Scriptures we see that the reference to a thousand years isn't speaking to a literal thousand years but to a large block of time. For this reason, and many others, I land solidly in the amillennial camp. This interpretation of Revelation 20 is a secondary issue, but it does shape and form us, so it's important.

Revelation 19:11–16 is the picture of Jesus we need right now, although it isn't a popular one.

> Then I saw heaven opened, and behold, a white horse! The one sitting on it is called Faithful and True, and in righteousness he judges and makes war. His eyes are like a flame of fire, and on his head are many diadems, and he has a name written that no one knows but himself. He is clothed in a robe dipped in blood [Note: this is Jesus' blood; there hasn't been a battle yet], and the name by which he is called is The Word of God. And the armies of heaven, arrayed in fine linen, white and pure, were following him on white horses.

There's so much here. Why are warriors dressed like priests in this big fight? Why are they dressed in white linen? You don't go to war in white linen. You go to war in armor. Why are they on white horses? Only the victor gets the white horse. Why is He sharing this victory with us?

> From his mouth comes a sharp sword with which to strike down the nations, and he will rule them with a rod of iron. He will tread

the winepress of the fury of the wrath of God the Almighty. On his robe and on his thigh he has a name written, King of kings and Lord of lords. (vv. 15–16)

The two prevailing images of Jesus Christ in the imaginations of most people are baby Jesus in the manger and, God help us, feather-haired Jesus who never says anything mean to anybody. "It's just Spirit sprinkles for everybody."

Here we see who King Jesus really is: terrifying and lovely, all-powerful and worthy. This is tattoo-on-the-thigh Jesus. This is the not-playing-around-anymore Jesus. This is "I have given you thousands of years to turn from the beasts and the Dragon and to come into the salvation that I've purchased for you with this blood that is all over My robe. You've chosen the beast. You've chosen the Dragon, and time is up."

This is Jesus who comes to reign and rule, not "everybody is going to be all right" Jesus.

We need to see this Jesus so we won't lash out at our enemies like it's all on us. The Bible says I should consider myself blessed because they hated my Savior first. We're able to endure as Overcomers and love those who despise us because we know this Jesus is coming, and He'll either extend grace to them like He did to me, praise God, or He's coming with His holy wrath to burn away what isn't pure and perfect.

This scene lets me love everyone and not treat anyone as my enemy. Jesus is the just judge, not me.

THE KINGDOM OF GOD IS HERE

In Mark 1:15 Jesus began His ministry by saying, "The time is fulfilled, and the kingdom of God is at hand; repent and believe the gospel."

Jesus, right out of the gate, was saying that Israel's long-awaited King was here. The rule and reign of God was incarnate as the Son of God took on flesh and dwelt among humankind. Wherever Jesus goes, He demonstrates the kingdom but also deploys it.

In Luke 10, Jesus sent out seventy-two disciples, and they were able to do the works of the kingdom. They came back rejoicing because "even the demons are subject to us in your name!" (v. 17). The kingdom was inaugurated in the coming of Jesus, and the disciples were given the authority of the kingdom over the powers and principalities in this present darkness.

In Matthew 12, we see what our invitation as Overcomers is from King Jesus. Jesus healed a man with a withered hand on the Sabbath, causing the Pharisees to hatch a plan to destroy Him. In verse 22, we see Jesus heal a blind and mute man by casting out a demon. This so disoriented and frustrated the Pharisees that they claimed Jesus was casting out demons by the power of Beelzebul, a prince among the demons. Jesus responded, and it's in His response that we see our opportunity as Overcomers. In verse 25, Jesus said:

> Every kingdom divided against itself is laid waste, and no city or house divided against itself will stand. And if Satan casts out Satan, he is divided against himself. How then will his kingdom stand? . . . But if it is by the Spirit of God that I cast out demons, then the kingdom of God has come upon you. Or how can someone enter a strong man's house and plunder his goods, unless he first binds the strong man? Then indeed he may plunder his house. (vv. 25–29)

Jesus' response gives us insight into how to understand the millennial reign described in Revelation 20. Jesus said the kingdom of God is here and the strong man has been bound. He said the healing of this man by casting out this demon was plunder, the strong man has been bound and this demonically oppressed soul was His, and that He was taking it back as a trophy of victory.

The thousand-year reign of Jesus is an image of the church age between Jesus' first coming and His ultimate return. In the meantime, the strong man is bound, and as Overcomers we're plundering the earth with King Jesus.

When was the last time we read about the Dragon? The beasts are a consistent piece in Revelation with their political and cultural power, but we haven't heard anything about the Dragon since Revelation 12. Why are we just hearing about cultural and political power and false religion? Where is the Dragon? The last time we saw him, he stood on the shores and called up these beasts.

Every attack was thwarted by God. Could it be that Satan is currently attacking the world like a Mafia boss in prison? Could it be that he can't do much but make some phone calls? This means, Overcomers, the world is ours for plundering.

There are 2.38 billion Christians in the world.[3] We aren't geographically centered anywhere. That sounds like some serious plunder. Have you ever thought of yourself as a trophy of God's grace? According to Colossians 1:13, you have been "delivered . . . from the domain of darkness and transferred . . . to the kingdom of his beloved Son."

You and I have been plundered by the enemy. We were born in sin and iniquity. When some Overcomer before us shared with us the good news of the kingdom, the Holy Spirit opened our eyes and filled our spirits, and now we join in with King Jesus, taking back what is rightfully His.

I know the word *plunder* might conjure up violent images, but this is violent stuff. It's important not to forget that we plunder with the weapons of compassion, mercy, grace, healing, power, evangelism, and hospitality. Those are the weapons of our warfare, but it is violent, and it's been given to us to share in the victory with Christ.

It was largely accepted in the twentieth century that secularism would ultimately drive out religion. People thought eventually we'd all just believe in science, and science would show us, "That's not really God. It's natural phenomenon."

The exact opposite has happened. About ten years ago, Pew Research found out the world is getting *more* religious, not less. Tim Keller wrote:

> Demographers tell us the twenty-first century will be less secular than the twentieth. There have been seismic religious shifts toward Christianity in sub-Saharan Africa and China while evangelicalism and Pentecostalism have grown exponentially in Latin America. Even in the United States the growth of the "nones" has been mainly among those who had been more nominal in their relationship to faith while the devoutly religious in the United States and Europe are growing.[4]

This is plunder. This is victory. The Christian faith isn't shrinking. It's shifting locations, and that's partly on us. I don't feel called into this fight because I think we're going to lose. I feel called into this fight because wherever I see brokenness, sin, loss, suffering, and anxiety, I want to plunder the strong man's property.

I want to take from him what ultimately belongs to the King of kings and Lord of lords, who is coming to take it all back. And in the space between, you and I have been given the Holy Spirit and have been given the Great Commission and the Great Commandment to love and to make disciples. I'm saying that every act of surrender and obedience to Jesus Christ is an act of plundering what the enemy thinks is his. Sometimes it looks as small as you apologizing to your kids and asking forgiveness, reminding them that you need Jesus just as much as they do. Sometimes it looks like you finally owning to your spouse that you have been cruel and not kind. That's all plunder.

Overcomers, don't shrink back now. This is what you've been uniquely wired and placed for—the eternal and global purpose of your life! From your neighborhood to the ends of the earth, the Dragon has been bound, and the people of God have been set free to plunder.

Things are not as they seem. We are not on our heels; the enemy is on his. Jesus looked at Peter and said, "I will build my church, and the gates of hell shall not prevail against it" (Matthew 16:18). Not the cannons of hell or the missiles of hell—the gates. Gates are defensive measures, not offensive weapons. Every act of obedience in your life is an act of defiance against a bound Dragon and his henchmen.

Let me give you a simple invitation as we close out this chapter: Get together with a group of Christian friends in the next couple of weeks with the sole purpose of feasting. If you're in a home group or Bible study group at church, that works. Don't put all this onto one person, and spread it out. Don't start at 8 p.m. Start early, move slow. Spend the night telling one another how and when Jesus saved you from your sins. Put a fifteen-minute cap on it so no one dominates the evening. Let there be a signal at ten minutes to let the person know to start wrapping it up.

Go around the room, and over good food and good drink, tell the story of redemption and watch what the presence of Jesus does among you. Watch how encouraging it is. Ask questions of one another. As people share about hurt, rejection, fears, or doubts, enter in and pray over them.

As a child, I was not comforted by the thought of eternity. I was taught that things would get really bad after the rapture and that we'd later spend forever singing on clouds as disembodied spirits. As we conclude with the final chapters of Revelation, we must remember the book is meant to encourage us in our walk with God. Chapters 21–22 show us our future in God's presence. Heaven will overlap with earth as the earth is renewed. The world we know now is only a fraction of how incredible it will be. Not only will the earth be renewed, but our bodies will be renewed as well. We will be released from our perishable, weak body and will be given an imperishable, immortal body that will not wear out or get sick. The world's ethnic diversity will continue as a reflection of God's continued creativity. We will also have a renewed reality. We will enjoy the good gift of work without the toil that resulted from the fall. But most of all, we will be in the eternal presence of Jesus. Our faith will be sight. As we conclude this book, I hope we are now able to see ourselves and the enemy for what they are. We were created for this time and place to help bring about God's purposes on the earth as we share the good news with others.

CHAPTER 12

ALL THINGS NEW

I grew up with two primary thoughts about my eternal future. The first thought was taught at the church where I was saved: there will be a rapture before things get really bad. Jesus will come back like Luke Skywalker in a spiritual X-wing starfighter and drop two proton torpedoes onto the earth, destroying it and all the enemies of God with it. The Christians will be gathered in heaven, in some ethereal plane, and worship Jesus forever.

The second thought was we will be disembodied spirits singing on some cloud with a harp.

If I'm honest, the thought of eternity wasn't a comfort. I tried to get my head around ten thousand years of singing with no time coming off the clock and thought that sounded awful.

I'm not trying to start a fight here, but I've come to believe that neither of these is the biblical picture of what waits for you and me in glory. There's a reason Paul said in Romans 8:18 that "the sufferings of this present time are not worth comparing" to future glory, and in Philippians 1:21 that "to die is gain."

To understand why Jesus believed that and lived so boldly, we need to look at the final two chapters of Revelation. These two chapters pull us forward as Overcomers. This is what awaits us. We are closer to this now than when we started reading this book.

Remember, the purpose of the book of Revelation is to embolden your confidence in the King of kings and Lord of lords, come what may. These final two chapters show us our future is in a literal, physical place with literal, physical people in the presence of the Creator God.

YOUR RENOVATED HOME

In 2004, ABC rolled out a show called *Extreme Makeover: Home Edition*. In the show Ty Pennington and his team would do a backstory on a family who lived in a house that had become dilapidated and, in some instances, unlivable. There were holes in walls and floors. Broken windows and doors that wouldn't shut from cracked foundations as well as mold damage, fire damage, and, in most cases, problems with rats and other critters. Ty and his team would send the families away on a two-week vacation and completely renovate, rebuild, and restore the home with special personal touches for each of the family members. This is what is coming for you and me.

Revelation 21 starts like this:

Then I saw a new heaven and a new earth, for the first heaven and the first earth had passed away, and the sea was no more. And I saw the holy city, new Jerusalem, coming down out of heaven from God, prepared as a bride adorned for her husband. And I heard a loud voice from the throne saying, "Behold, the dwelling place of God is with man. He will dwell with them, and they will be his people, and God himself will be with them as their God. He will wipe away every tear from their eyes, and death shall be no more, neither shall there be mourning, nor crying, nor pain anymore, for the former things have passed away." (vv. 1–4)

The first thing to notice in this passage is that heaven comes down. It's not that you and I go somewhere else. In chapter 4, we talked about a convergent space where the presence of Jesus enthroned breaks into our reality. We saw that, throughout the Bible, heaven and earth overlap. In the tabernacle and temple, in the incarnation, and in the believer through the indwelling Holy Spirit, that picture of the throne comes down.

Wherever the people of God dial into heaven, we get these glimpses, these tastes, these moments where that reality breaks through. Revelation 21:1–4 says all that just comes down and lands. It's not some sort of ethereal, otherworldly, escapist reality. You're not going to get rescued out of a broken world. The broken world will be redeemed, and you'll stay. When we look at verses 9–21, we see materiality everywhere: gates, walls, a river, and trees that bear fruit in season. The language in the passage is still apocalyptic but describes a literal, physical location. The world we're in remains.

The passage says the first heaven and earth had passed away (v. 1), and 2 Peter 3:10 says, "The heavens will pass away with a roar, and the heavenly bodies will be burned up and dissolved, and the earth and the works that are done on it will be exposed."

In both instances, this isn't a reference to the destruction of the earth but its renewal. The Greek word translated "new" is *kainos*, meaning "new in nature or in quality." In other words, when these passages employ the phrase "new heaven and new earth," they teach a world *renewed*, not a world brand-new. Therefore, what we see in the Scripture's vision of the end of redemptive history isn't an earth thrown in the trash can with its righteous inhabitants escaping to disembodied bliss in the clouds; instead, we see a restored earth where creation has been reconciled to God.

The Bible consistently points to a world remade by the coming glory of God. Isaiah prophesied that the deserts will bloom with roses, that there will be no more weeping heard on the earth, that the days of God's people shall be like the days of the tree, and that the wolf and the lamb will lie down together. The lion will chew straw like the oxen. This is the world renewed and the world remade. The prophet Amos said the plowman shall overtake the reaper, and the mountains shall drip sweet wine (9:13). Habbakuk joined in and said the earth will be filled with the knowledge of the Lord as waters cover the sea (2:14). Paul taught that even nonhuman creation will join in the redemption of the children of God (Romans 8:19–22).

God isn't going to concede the earth to His enemies. The incarnation is Jesus showing up in this physical place and saying, "This is Mine." The resurrection is a reminder that the earth is the Lord's and everything in it (Acts 17:24). It is His, and it is our inheritance.

George Eldon Ladd said "The Bible always places men and women on a redeemed earth, not in a heavenly realm removed from earthly existence. God will not concede the earth to the enemy. It will be remade. It will be renewed."[1]

After I finished my last round of chemotherapy in 2011, I wondered if I'd ever feel physically strong again. An opportunity to hike the Inca Trail and see Machu Picchu came up, and I jumped on it. For nine months, I pushed my body as hard as I could in preparation. The hike would be four days and three nights. I landed in Cusco, Peru, excited to start the journey. The trail crosses four ecozones, each with differing microclimates. So each day there were new flowers, climates, and views to drink in.

On the last day, we woke up while it was still dark to make it to the Sun Gate before the sun crested over the Andes. As the sun poured over the jagged tops of the mountains, I sat there stunned by the beauty of it all. I thought of a quote from my ancient friend Augustine, who said, "If these are the beauties afforded to sinful men, what does God have in store for those who love him?"[2]

Here's what I want the Spirit to do every time you see an epic sunset, the kind that paints the sky all sorts of wild colors. For the rest of your life, I want you to think, *That's incredible, but not as incredible as it will be.* When you go to the mountains or the ocean or you finally get to see the Grand Canyon or another physical place that stirs up your affections, I'd love for the Spirit of God to just roll to the front of your mind: *That's incredible, and it's not half of what it will be.*

Our future as Overcomers isn't life on a cloud in some ethereal plane. It's in a literal, physical location, and we'll be there in physical bodies.

YOUR RENEWED BODY

At the time of this writing, I'm eighteen days away from my forty-eighth birthday. I try to take good care of myself physically. I work out several times a week and try to make good choices about what I eat. Despite my efforts, I still woke up this morning with stiff hips and neck. All I did was sleep. At my age, one of the more dangerous things I can do is sleep on the wrong kind of pillow.

The last chapter of Ecclesiastes teaches that if we live long enough, everything about our physical bodies will stop working, wear out, and break. In 1 Corinthians 15:35–58, the apostle Paul told us our physical bodies are perishable, dishonorable, and weak. Paul wasn't only teaching that but also letting us know that our current bodies can't survive in the full presence of God. This goes back to the holiness of God. Our earthen bodies will be dissolved in the full brilliance of God's presence. To abide with Him, we'll need a redeemed and renewed body.

Paul told us we will be given an imperishable and immortal body either at the resurrection or the return of Jesus. It's in these physical bodies that we will dwell in the new heaven and earth. We'll see with new physical eyes, hear with actual ears, taste, touch, and smell with renewed nostrils. I'm not sure what these bodies will look like, but we do know they can't get sick, grow weary, wear out, or die.

Revelation 21:3 adds another piece to the physicality of our new bodies. The people of God are being gathered from among the full range of the world's ethnic diversity: every tribe, tongue, and nation. In the same way God doesn't destroy material stuff, He doesn't destroy the peoples. Various ethnicities aren't a problem solved by new resurrection bodies; they are an expression of God's creative beauty. No one ethnicity and no one culture can bear the brunt or the weight of the breadth and beauty of the Creator God of the universe.

The next part of the picture is what we'll be doing in this renewed earth with our renewed bodies.

RENEWED REALITY

It usually took me two to three weeks to fully recover from a round of chemotherapy. After my last dose wore off, I simply got back to work. I felt great and was filled with gratitude that it looked like I'd survive much longer than the initial prognosis. I was preaching again. I was leading in the rooms I was meant to lead in. I was starting to write books again and trying to step into what God had for me. I could feel my days were numbered, and I wanted to maximize them.

About three years after my last dose of chemo, I woke up with a humming, frenetic energy. No coffee needed. I felt like someone had given me a shot of B12. It was clean energy with no back edge. It was like I shifted into a gear I didn't know I hadn't been using for the past three years.

Then, all of a sudden, I remembered, *Yeah! I used to be like this.* For years, I hadn't been operating at my full capacity. It had been taken from me by surgery, the poison of chemotherapy, and an anti-seizure medication that I thankfully was able to wean off with my doctor's help.

In our everyday lives this side of glory, we eat, sleep, work, play, rest, travel, and manage the daily dramas of being alive. On the renewed earth in our renewed bodies, much of this will continue but with a strength we've never known before. Throughout the Scriptures, it's said that you and I will rule and reign alongside King Jesus in the new heavens and earth (2 Timothy 2:11–13; Romans 5:12–21; Ephesians 2:1–7) and even that we will judge angels and rule over cities (Luke 19:17, 19). That means we won't just be playing a harp and singing. We will be kings and queens serving the ultimate King. Revelation 21:24 says, "By its light will the nations walk, and the kings of the earth will bring their glory into it." You and I, in our resurrected bodies (1 Corinthians 15:51–54), will reign and rule in this place alongside King Jesus. Now, I don't know what that reigning and ruling actually entails, other than it looks like we have jobs—jobs without toil.

Work is a good gift, but sin pollutes it with toil. Adam and Eve were given massive jobs, and they loved, delighted, and rejoiced in these jobs until sin entered the cosmos. Then sin fractured the good gift of work. Genesis 3:18 says that, as a result of the fall, work produces thorns and thistles now, and from the sweat of your brow, you'll take from the earth. In the renewed heaven and earth, this has been restored. Work stays, but toil is gone.

With this said, could it be in this passage that the phrase "kings of the earth" (Revelation 21:24) is a reference to the people of God who are reigning and ruling alongside Jesus Christ?

Kings in the first century weren't just rulers, but they embodied the nation's culture, which they carried with them. If you wanted to know what a nation believed about education, you needed only to see its king. If you wanted to know whether it was a warrior culture or an agrarian culture, you needed only to look at their king. If you want to know what the culture believes about family dynamics, look to the king.

In Revelation 21:24, we have a quick little verse that's saying there's a literal, redeemed, remade, physical location—a new heavens and new earth—and "the kings of earth." I think that's a reference to you and me. We're carrying our trophies or beauties of our culture into this new reality to be enjoyed by all.

As I've traveled around the world, I've marveled at the varying values and cultural artifacts that other people groups embrace. I've learned that in certain cultures my personality type can be problematic. I'm loud, I value physical touch, and I've never met a stranger. In my experience, Brazil, Italy, and parts of Africa are places where that fits in beautifully.

In other places, I need to press the brakes on my natural enthusiasm so as not to be unintentionally offensive. There are varying styles of music, food, dress, senses of humor, and ways of celebrating. According to Revelation 21, the redeemed and renewed aspects of every culture are brought into the New Jerusalem.

Theologian Anthony Hoekema asked these questions concerning the new heaven and new earth:

> Will there be "better Beethoven" on the new earth . . . better Rembrandts, better Raphaels . . . ? Shall we read better poetry, better drama, and better prose? Will scientists continue to advance in

technological achievement? Will geologists continue to dig out the treasures of the earth, and will architects continue to build imposing and attractive structures? Will there be exciting new adventures in space travel?[3]

In the new heaven and new earth, there is work, there is culture, and there is feasting without any toil. On top of all this, we see in Revelation 21:1 that there is no sea. To men and women across biblical times, the sea stood for chaos. They were terrified of the sea. They wouldn't want to go near the sea. It was unknown. It was chaotic. In the remade heaven and earth, there is no chaos.

Can you imagine no chaos—not just in your life but in the world? It's hard to get my mind around a world without chaos. It's always there in my house, at my office, on the freeway, or on an airplane to wherever. But not here. There will be no chaos.

Now look at verse 4: No tears. No death. No disease. No mourning. No crying. Imagine a reality in which no one is sick. No one is sad. No one is crying about anything. There's literally nothing to mourn. The passage also says the "former things have passed away" (v. 4). No regrets, no heartache, no shame. All things made new.

This all sounds incredible, but we haven't covered the best thing about the future glory that awaits us as Overcomers.

PRESENCE

The ever-increasing joy of the renewed earth, physical bodies, and reality isn't that the sunsets are prettier, or that we're not struggling in our jobs, or that there are no more tears, death, disease, or loss. No. The reward is the presence of Jesus—unblocked, unfettered, with nothing to keep us from seeing Him completely. Faith will be sight.

In Revelation 21:22, John said, "And I saw no temple in the city, for its temple is the Lord God the Almighty and the Lamb." If we were reading this as a Jewish man or woman in AD 96, we would've gasped at that idea. No temple? Where do you commune with God? Where do you get in His presence? How do you get to the place you were literally designed to dwell? In biblical times, you went to the temple. It was where God chose to dwell.

Remember, once a year the great high priest would go in to make atonement, and only one guy once a year got to go into the cubed-shaped holy of holies. Did anybody pay attention to how this new reality is shaped? Did anybody realize it is shaped like a cube? Where else do we read about the cube? In Solomon's temple in the holy of holies.

In the new heaven and new earth, the whole world has become the holy of holies. In this new reality, you and I are positioned as physical bodies in a physical place in the holy of holies. We're ushered right into the middle of the heart of the triune God of the universe. Our whole experience on the earthly side of things has been from the outside, looking up. We have a little bit of the glory of God in us, about as much as this little physical body can have without exploding. In this new reality, we step right into the middle of the triune God of the universe—in the middle of all that love and all that power—and it just blows our new reality into the stratosphere.

To dwell in the middle of the Trinity in the middle of that perfect love and in the middle of that power is what makes all this extraordinary. I'd argue that if you could live forever but you couldn't be in His presence, then you wouldn't want to live forever. You've already experienced this—things get old to you. Why don't things get old here? Because Jesus is an inexhaustible well, and you get to slip right into the middle of it, which is why the apostle Paul said it's going to take the coming ages for you to understand the depth of God's grace and mercy for us (Romans 11:33). In fact, this vision of the future is what helps you understand the verses from Paul I mentioned earlier: "I consider that the sufferings of this present time are not worth comparing with the glory that is to be revealed to us" (Romans 8:18). And "to live is Christ, and to die is gain" (Philippians 1:21). This is what Paul was looking at.

When this is our future hope and each passing hour and day gets us closer, our courage grows. What can other humans actually do? Mock us? Fire us from our jobs? Call us names? Put us in prison? This is where we're headed. Darrell Johnson said, "We will finally live, consciously so, within the circle of the inner Trinitarian relations of God. We mere creatures and creation itself will be drawn into the circle of holy love that has forever existed as Father, Son, and Holy Spirit."[4]

To be invited right into the very core of the Godhead—and not just us, but all creation—so that we live, dwell, and have our being in that place for eternity. This isn't clouds and harps. This is reigning and ruling in resurrected bodies alongside our King and Savior in His inexhaustible well of joy and goodness for eternity.

FACE-TO-FACE

In January 1999, I asked an eighteen-year-old Lauren Walker to marry me. We'd been dating for about a year and a half, and I knew I wanted to spend my life with her. We originally planned to be married in December close to her parents' anniversary, but we switched the date to July as we both realized we weren't made for a long engagement. After six months of waiting, on July 31, 1999, I stood at the front of the First Baptist Church in Longview, Texas, and impatiently waited to see Lauren walk down the aisle toward me.

I'd seen Lauren the night before, but I had an ache in my heart to see her in that space. I longed to enter the covenant of marriage with her. To promise God and her in front of our family and friends that, regardless of poverty or riches, sickness or health, joy or sorrow, I'd be hers and hers only—in mind, heart, and body—until death separates us. I watched as eight beautiful, godly women came down the aisle. Each was lovely, passionate about Jesus, and would have made an excellent bride, but none of them was Lauren Walker.

As the bridesmaids settled in, the room grew quiet. As music began to swell in the sanctuary, the back doors swung open—and there she was, looking radiant. I would kiss her mouth, and we would be declared husband and wife. I can still remember the visceral anticipation I felt that day.

Revelation 22:4 says, "They will see his face." I've been following Jesus Christ for thirty years. That's a long time. I've rejoiced with Him, wept with Him, felt undone in His presence. I've wrestled with Him and argued with Him. In all my foolishness, Jesus has never forsaken me. I've been protected by Him, defended by Him, and rescued by Him more times than I know. Jesus has redeemed my bloodline. He has held me fast. In the darkest moments of my life, He was right there. I've prayed immature and embarrassing prayers and have consistently fallen short of what Jesus has for me. After all these years, I'm still slow to obey and stunted in many areas of my life—and I'm going to see Him face-to-face.

You're going to see Him face-to-face too. And on that day, what we will hear is "Well done."

Can you believe that? Do you feel like you've done a good job? I'm aware of my shortcomings and the times I foolishly refused to obey or stumbled. We will see Him face-to-face, and there will be no condemnation for us, no eye roll, no loaded questions like "What were you thinking?" No.

We will see Him face-to-face. "Well done. Enter into your reward."

In every way, by the grace of God, we should be living for this moment. Seeing Jesus face-to-face orients the Christian life. Each moment is seen as a step toward this ultimate destiny. Each day, week, month, year, and decade is seen as a pilgrimage to this great end. This is the eternal bliss that awaits the Overcomers.

AN INVITATION

Look at the invitation in Revelation 22:17: "The Spirit and the Bride say, 'Come.' And let the one who hears say, 'Come.' And let the one who is thirsty come; let the one who desires take the water of life without price." Let's consider this invitation as we close out our study of Revelation together.

I want you to pay attention to the capital *S* in this passage. That capital *S* in "Spirit" means we're talking about the third person of the Trinity—God the Spirit. God the Spirit says, "Come. Have a seat. Drink the water of life without price." The same God who called you to Himself is now calling your friends, family, neighbors, and others around you into His rest, peace, and salvation. As we live as Overcomers, it's important to remember this is God's invitation, God's mission, and ultimately His salvation. We are His ambassadors, but He is the Savior, and He invites all to Himself.

But look who He is making the appeal through. Did you notice who else is saying, "Come"? The bride of Christ (v. 17). That's us. That's *you*! The church.

As this book is landing, what is Jesus saying? The Spirit and the bride continually invite those outside-the-kingdom people to come inside the kingdom and pull up a chair. This is yet another invitation to sit and eat.

UNVEILED

Mike May was three years old when a jar of chemicals exploded in his face, leaving him blind. Despite his blindness, May went on to work for the CIA, became a successful entrepreneur, and even holds the world record for downhill speed skiing for a completely blind person. In 2000, May's sight was partially restored by a pioneering transplant using stem cells. Although he needed to wear what we would consider binoculars to see crisply, the world began to come in view as he was able to see what was there. The more he saw, the more old fears melted away.

Mike told the story of a waterfall near Lake Tahoe that could frighten him. He wrote, "Up close to these particular falls, I could not understand what someone was saying more than two feet away. Over 30 feet away, it is not likely that I would hear a person yelling. It frightened me that my kids could get in trouble and I wouldn't even know."

With his sight restored, he speaks of the same place but with more courage and confidence: "This time was different. I put the binoculars to my face and all sorts of things I could barely see came leaping into view. The water, which sounds so intimidating, looked soft and bubbly. Best of all I could see Carson and Wyndham happily climbing on the rocks. Even though Jennifer was nearby, I felt safe knowing where they were myself and it was fun to see them exploring."[5]

If you remember, in chapter 2 we said the word *apocalypse* means "unveiling." I pray at this point in the book, with these last few moments we are spending together, that you would see—like Mike May did—with the veil partially removed, and now some of the things that were scary and disorienting when we started no longer hold much power over you.

In the time it took me to write this book, there have been multiple mass shootings, a massive wave of violence has erupted in the Middle East, depression and anxiety have skyrocketed, multiple well-known pastors have been publicly disqualified, and an entire denomination's evil has been brought into the light.

Our culture is being torn apart by fear and anger, by a broken system and an algorithm that keeps us in an echo chamber, and by media with much to gain financially by keeping us afraid and angry. The tension over politics, race, and gender has subsided some as I finish the book, but it's just under the surface, ready to explode again at the next opportunity.

The two henchmen of the Dragon are making war against the people of God and deceiving much of humankind along the way. It's a giant, painful, awful mess.

But, like Mike May, you see more clearly now. You see yourself and the enemy's schemes for what they are. You were born for this specific moment. No more idleness or shrinking back from you. This is your day. You were made for it, and it was made for you.

You now know the enemy has lost and is simply thrashing about in the final moments of his life. Along with your massive multicultural, multiethnic global family, you lament the destruction, pain, and loss sin causes but that moves you toward the fight, not from it. You are a warrior saint wielding the truth of God's Word, empowered by the Holy Spirit, and holding fast to the victory of Jesus that is in place now. You don't have to be quiet or neutral, because you know we are not on our heels, but the enemy is on his.

I know you will live humbly but in boldness because the strong man is bound and there's much to be plundered in the peoples of the earth. I'm so grateful God placed you in your neighborhood and wove into you the aptitudes and desires that led you to your job. I'm grateful the Spirit goes with you to the gym where you work out and the coffee shop where you get your drink.

You were made for the day, and the day was made for you. You were uniquely wired by God and placed right where you are as an Overcomer! I'm cheering you on from Dallas.

We have the enemy right where we want him—on his heels.

THE OVERCOMERS MANIFESTO

We covered a lot of ground in the book, and I know living it will be different than reading it. Here at the very end, I want to remind you what you are and then provide a manifesto of sorts to strengthen you when you find yourself losing perspective, feeling defeated, or forgetting about that throne Jesus is sitting on right now and you have access to.

In Christ Jesus I am not a victim but an Overcomer.
I was made for this day, and this day was made for me.
I am uniquely wired by God and placed right where I am
    by Him for service to Him.
I see reality for what it is, and I live courageously.
I lament the destruction sin causes in this world, and I
    cling to my security found in Jesus.

I hold on to Him with total surrender, and I stand with
Him as a stabilizing, unanxious presence amid
this immoral and chaotic world.

In the power of the Spirit, I zealously pray for all that
God puts before me.

I am well aware of the enemy and know that, in Jesus, I
am a major problem to him.

That is okay; I fight back.

Along with God's people, I wage war with the truth of His
Word, with confession, and with a life of worship.

I am not idle.

Seriously pursuing a ferocious holiness, I kill my sins by
dragging them into His light.

Standing on the promises of God, I trust that Jesus has
accomplished everything I need to flourish.

I see God's image bearers who are trapped, and I
join His rescue mission in the offensive against
darkness and destruction.

This is a cosmic war.

In Him, I am not shaken.

Since the strong man is bound, I plunder the earth with
King Jesus for the souls of men and women.

Through radically ordinary hospitality, I will proclaim
the gospel where God has placed me.

I am under His mercy, at His table, delighting in His
goodness and grace.

One day, in a literal, physical location and in my physical
body, I will see Jesus face-to-face and hear Him
say, "Well done."

I will not shrink back now, because Christ compels me forward.

I am not a victim; I am an Overcomer.

ACKNOWLEDGMENTS

Even though it is my name on the cover of this book, it was born in and through a community of people. I want to start by thanking Lauren, the wife of my youth and the one who has to endure my seasons of hyperfixation. Your voice and insight are woven throughout the pages of this book. To my children Audrey, Reid, and Norah, thank you for allowing me to set up in "the middle of everything" to write this book. To the river cabin crew: Elizabeth Woodson, Mason King, Trevor Joy, Lindsey Eenigenburg, Jen Wilkin, and Kent Rabalais. Talking through and arguing around the book of Revelation in the fall of 2020 both shaped the conviction and ultimately the content of this book. To my assistant, Andrea Bowman, for organizing and optimizing my world so I can run hard into my calling. To Curtis and Karen Yates for their friendship and help. This book is better for your insights, encouragement, and constant teaching. To the W Publishing team, thank you for your exceptional skills in bringing this book to life and loving Jesus and the Scriptures the way you do. Thank you to Eugene Peterson, Darrell Johnson, David Campbell and G. K. Beale for your works on Revelation. Each of them stretched, encouraged, and emboldened my own soul. Lastly to the elders of The Village Church, thank you for allowing me to serve alongside you the beautiful people of TVC. Love standing shield to shield with you.

NOTES

Introduction

1. "James J. Braddock," Estate of James J. Braddock, accessed November 8, 2023, https://www.jamesjbraddock.com.

Chapter 1

1. For the purpose of this chapter, I am using the term *general identity* to talk about what is true of all believers everywhere. Later in the chapter, we will talk about our specific identities, which are tied to our being uniquely wired and uniquely placed by God.
2. John 1:12; 8:36; 15:15; 1 Corinthians 3:16–17; 2 Corinthians 5:17; Philippians 3:20; Ephesians 2:10; Galatians 2:20; 4:7; 1 John 3:1; 4:4.
3. John Newton and Richard Cecil, *Memoirs of the Rev. John Newton*, in *The Works of the Rev. John Newton* (Edinburgh: Banner of Truth, 1985), 1:107.

Chapter 2

1. *A Thief in the Night*, directed by Donald W. Thompson (Des Moines, IA: Mark IV Pictures, 1973), film.
2. We will take a chapter-by-chapter view of Revelation rather than a line-by-line deep dive.

3. Eugene Peterson, *Reversed Thunder: The Revelation of John and the Praying Imagination* (San Francisco: Harper & Row, 1988), xi–xii.

4. David Campbell, *Mystery Explained: A Simple Guide to Revelation* (n.p.: David Campbell, 2016), 26.

5. Darrell Johnson, *Discipleship on the Edge: An Expository Journey Through the Book of Revelation* (Vancouver, BC: Regent College Publishing, 2004), 22.

6. *The Lord of the Rings: The Two Towers*, directed by Peter Jackson (New Line Cinema, 2002), film.

Chapter 3

1. *The Lord of the Rings: The Two Towers*, directed by Peter Jackson (New Line Cinema, 2002), film.

2. Francis A. Schaeffer, *No Little People* (Wheaton, IL: Crossway, 2003), 79.

Chapter 4

1. Barry Bobb, *All God's People Sing* (St. Louis: Concordia Publishing House, 1992), 316.

2. G. K. Beale, *The Book of Revelation: A Commentary on the Greek Text* (Grand Rapids, MI: Eerdmans, 1998), 329.

3. John Calvin, *The Institutes of Christian Religion* (Princeton, NJ: Princeton University Press, 1541).

4. Eugene Peterson, *Reversed Thunder: The Revelation of John and the Praying Imagination* (San Francisco: Harper & Row, 1988), 59.

5. Robert Robinson, "Come Thou Fount of Every Blessing," 1758, public domain.

6. Peterson, *Reversed Thunder*, 61.

7. Peterson, *Reversed Thunder*, 62.

8. N. T. Wright, *Simply Christian: Why Christianity Makes Sense* (New York: HarperOne, 2010), 157.

Chapter 5

1. Tim Keller, *Walking with God through Pain and Suffering* (New York: Penguin Books, 2015).

2. Marina Pitofsky, "Rage Rooms: Why Recreational Smashing Could Be Good for Your Mental Health," *USA Today*, November 11, 2018, https://www.usatoday.com/story/news/2018/11/11/rage-rooms-what-might-surprise-you-growing-trend/1754653002.

3. Elijah del Medigo, "Only a God Can Save Us," The American Mind, May 11, 2020, https://americanmind.org/features/the-green-zone-plan /only-a-god-can-save-us.

4. Peterson, *Reversed Thunder*, 84.

5. "Sing All Along the Way," Music Notes, Inc., accessed November 8, 2023, https://www.musicyoucanread.com/SONGS/03-SINGA.html.

Chapter 6

1. W. A. Elwell and B. J. Beitzel, *Baker Encyclopedia of the Bible* (Grand Rapids, MI: Baker, 1988), 2:1784.

2. Darrell Johnson, *Discipleship on the Edge: An Expository Journey Through the Book of Revelation* (Vancouver, BC: Regent College Publishing, 2004), 195.

3. David Campbell, *Mystery Explained: A Simple Guide to Revelation* (DC Christian Publishing, 2021), 75.

4. Martin Luther, *Luther's Ninety-Five Theses* (Phillipsburg, NJ: P&R Publishing, 2017).

5. Richard Lovelace, *Dynamics of Spiritual Life: An Evangelical Theology of Renewal* (Downers Grove, IL: InterVarsity Press, 1979), 160.

6. E. M. Bounds, *Power through Prayer* (New York: Simon & Schuster, 2011).

Chapter 7

1. You can find Jennie's interview at ifgathering.com or search for "Sheep Among Wolves" on YouTube.

2. Jonathan Leeman, "Essential and Indispensable: Women and the Mission of the Church," 9Marks, December 10, 2019, https://www.9marks.org/article/ essential-and-indispensable-women-and-the-mission-of-the-church.

3. Tim Keller, *The Reason for God* (Dutton, 2008).

Chapter 8

1. *The Princess Bride,* directed by Rob Reiner, 20th Century Studios (Metro-Goldwyn-Mayer, Lionsgate, Vestron Pictures, 1987), film.

2. G. K. Beale with David H. Campbell, *Revelation: A Shorter Commentary* (Grand Rapids, MI: Eerdmans, 2015), 454.

3. Tim Chester, *You Can Change* (Wheaton, IL: Crossway, 2013).

4. "We Touch Our Smartphones at Least 2,617 Times a Day!," *Economic Times,* last updated July 14, 2016, https://economictimes.indiatimes

.com/magazines/panache/we-touch-our-smartphones-at-least-2617
-times-a-day/articleshow/53211326.cms.

5. Erwin van der Meer, "The Strategic Level Spiritual Warfare Theology of C. Peter Wagner and Its Implications for Christian Mission in Malawi," Academia, November 2008, https://www.academia.edu/8022071/The_strategic_level_spiritual_warfare_theology_of_C_Peter_Wagner_and_its_implications_for_Christian_mission_in_Malawi.

6. Rosaria Butterfield, *The Gospel Comes with a House Key* (Wheaton, IL: Crossway, 2018), 40.

7. Stephen Rhodes, *Where the Nations Meet: The Church in a Multicultural World* (Downers Grove, IL: InterVarsity Press, 1998), 135.

Chapter 9

1. Conrad Hackett and David McClendon, "Christians Remain World's Largest Religious Group, but They are Declining in Europe," Pew Research, April 5, 2017, https://www.pewresearch.org/short-reads/2017/04/05/christians-remain-worlds-largest-religious-group-but-they-are-declining-in-europe.

2. "Harp," Vienna Symphonic Library, accessed November 8, 2023, https://www.vsl.info/en/academy/strings/harp#sound-characteristics.

3. "Suicide Statistics," American Foundation for Suicide Prevention, accessed November 8, 2023, https://afsp.org/suicide-statistics.

4. J. I. Packer, *Knowing God* (Wheaton, IL: Crossway, 2023).

5. Darrell Johnson, *Discipleship on the Edge* (Vancouver: Regent College, 2004), 253–66.

6. Johnson, *Discipleship on the Edge*, 270.

Chapter 10

1. Michael P. Zuckert, "Madison's Consistency on the Bill of Rights," National Affairs, 2021, https://www.nationalaffairs.com/publications/detail/madisons-consistency-on-the-bill-of-rights.

2. Mark Trainer, "What Does it Mean for a Right to be Inalienable?," Share America, July 25, 2018, https://share.america.gov/what-does-it-mean-for-right-to-be-inalienable.

3. Thomas F. Torrance, *Apocalypse Today* (James Clark Lutterworth, 1961), 130.

4. J. R. R. Tolkien, *The Hobbit* (George Allen & Unwin, 1937), chap. 5.

5. Tolkien, *The Fellowship of the Ring* (George Allen & Unwin, 1937), chap. 2.

Chapter 11

1. Peterson, *Reversed Thunder*, 166–67.

2. Augustine, *The Confessions of St. Augustine Bishop of Hippo* (New York: Simon & Schuster, 2013).

3. "Religion by Country 2023," World Population Review, https://worldpopulationreview.com/country-rankings/religion-by-country.

4. Timothy Keller and Sean Pratt, *Making Sense of God: An Invitation to the Skeptical* (New York: Penguin, 2016), 10–11.

Chapter 12

1. George Eldon Ladd, *The Gospel of the Kingdom* (Grand Rapids, MI: Eerdmans, 1990).

2. Augustine, *City of God* (New York: Simon & Schuster, 1958).

3. Anthony A. Hoekema, *The Bible and the Future* (Grand Rapids, MI: Eerdmans, 1994).

4. Johnson, *Discipleship on the Edge*, 372.

5. Mike May, "The Trees Were a Deeper Green Than I Imagined, and So Tall," *The Guardian*, August 25, 2003, https://www.theguardian.com/science/2003/aug/26/genetics.g2.

ABOUT THE AUTHOR

Matt Chandler is a husband, father, pastor, elder, and author whose greatest desire is to make much of Jesus. He has served over twenty years as the lead pastor at The Village Church in Flower Mound, Texas, which recently transitioned its five campuses into their own autonomous churches. He is also the executive chairman of the Acts 29 Network, a large church-planting community that trains and equips church planters across the globe.

Matt is known around the world for proclaiming the gospel in a powerful and down-to-earth way and enjoys traveling to share the message of Jesus whenever he can. He lives in Texas with his beautiful wife, Lauren, and their three children, Audrey, Reid, and Norah.